George R. Moore

Bible Views of Creation

George R. Moore

Bible Views of Creation

ISBN/EAN: 9783337171827

Printed in Europe, USA, Canada, Australia, Japan

Cover: Foto ©Lupo / pixelio.de

More available books at **www.hansebooks.com**

BIBLE VIEWS OF CREATION.

BIBLE VIEWS
OF
CREATION

BY
REV. GEORGE R. MOORE

PHILADELPHIA
JOHN McGILL WHITE AND COMPANY
1328 Chestnut Street.

Copyrighted 1895
BY GEORGE R. MOORE
All Rights Reserved.

TO BIBLE STUDENTS.

****

To BIBLE STUDENTS the following pages are respectfully dedicated.

G. R. M.

Science is the reading aright the revelations of God in nature and the Bible.

Nothing is scientific that is out of harmony with any truth from any source.

"Consider the lillies of the field."—Matt. 6:28.

"And this is life eternal, that they might know thee the only true God, and Jesus Christ, whom thou hast sent."—John, 17:3.

Bible Views of Creation.

****

"In the beginning God created the heaven and the earth."—Gen. i : 1.

"By the word of the Lord were the heavens made, and all the host of them by the breath of his mouth."—Ps. xxxiii : 6.

"Through faith we understand that the worlds were framed by the word of God, so that things which are seen were not made of things which do appear."—Heb. xi : 3.

The Bible does not make the mistake of alluding to our world as of a separate creation from the other parts of the universe. It presents the universe as the creation of God in unity, and then the earth for our special consideration.

Having said that the heaven and the earth was the creation of God "at the beginning," the next information given us relates to the earth's substance as it was then known to have been before any change or transformations were set in motion within it (that created substance), so as to make it discoverable as a visible world. In its first stage of being, and prior to its second stage of being, " it was without form and void."

"All visible nature is a multifarious association of very compound substances, of which the particles must have been in some other state before they were compounded together. The simple condition of the elements must have preceded their union in the compound, and thus it is physically impossible that a compound can have been eternal. Composition and eternity are as incompatible as to be and not to be."—Turner.

It is equally clear that the elements thus spoken of were not visible prior to their being compounded, and hence that all visible things are of a later formation than the invisible, and "that the things that are seen were not made of things that do appear."—Heb. xi: 3.

"**And** the **earth** was without form, and void."

—Genesis, 1:2.

SEEN AND UNSEEN.

CHAPTER I.

I see here a blade of grass. I am curious to know what it is and how it came here. Whether it is simple or compound. What are the elements in it? How did it become a blade of grass? I see that it is a material thing. What I see and feel are certainly matter, but where did it come from? And what was the shape of this matter when it was being worked up into this blade of grass?

Not seen here three days ago, and now such a clean, tiny thing it is! I look another day, and lo! my blade of grass is twenty times as high as it was when I saw it before, and I say: "How fast it grows." What is it to grow? It has twenty times as much matter in it now as it had before.

I cannot see one atom of this matter as it

is taking its place in this spear of grass and causing it to grow. These materials are in some way being invisibly placed where we now see them. The matter itself could not be seen until it became grass. As a seen thing this grass has come from things unseen.

I look upon the carpet in my room and think of the wool in it as it was once seen growing on a sheep's back in the pasture. Our spear of grass may have helped this wool-making, but not until it was eaten up by the sheep and thoroughly digested and well circulated in the animal's fluids, and then by some invisible selections of the invisible atoms required to make the wool grow, it came out upon the surface of the sheep's body as a seen thing from atoms that a little time before were unseen.

I notice the paper upon which I am writing. What is it? It is fibrous material, wrought out in some way into these thin, smooth sheets of paper. Fiber is always a product of some living thing that grows; it may have come from the cotton plant, or it may be of wood growth, or flax, or of some other growth of fiber made by a vegetable or animal life in some past time and in some other form than it now presents to us. As a seen thing all of its material atoms have once or more passed through a state of growing in which they were unseen.

I look upon the table I am using to write upon. Most of it is made of wood; but there is no wood in the world, or knowledge that any has ever existed in it, that did not become a seen thing by growing as the trees about us are now doing, invisibly increasing their bulk as the blades of grass do.

If now we question any other visible thing simply to find the original state of its material atoms, our progress will be towards invisible fluids, and we shall find by exact history and careful analysis that the final material elements out of, and by which, all things seen are made have been in some previous time invisible atoms in a fluid state.

And no exception to be made to this statement as a universal truth. There is nothing in all the world about us, of things organized or unorganized, that does not bring to our minds the clear testimony that its visible form comes of the assembling or collecting of material atoms that somewhere existed before in a fluid and invisible state.

I am not speaking now of what it is that has changed the fluid atoms and made some of them into visible things, but simply of the fact that they have been changed, or collected, and are now held together in making what is seen out of the unseen.

Our visible world has all come out to view by reason of changes from a former state of its own elements, in which it was an unseen existence and its elements were free in space and of such variety and number as Infinite Wisdom chose to use, or to provide for His intended use in the making of things visible for this world and probably for all worlds.

A perfect analysis of any solid shows its elements to be of fluid descent. The granulation and crystallization of rocks and metals bears witness to **the same** thing **as clearly and certainly as a cake of ice bears witness** to its former condition as **water.** There was liquid before crystallization and fluid before liquid. But without actual analysis we find the atoms singly are quite **too** small **to be** visible. **No single** atom of matter has **ever** been seen, hence by reason we know if they **were** liberated from cohesion and **each one to go free in space,** solids would again pass to a fluid state and **be obedient to the law of** repulsion. **There would then be no visible things** anywhere. **The atoms of the world, in** that state, would be **spread out in space,** floating among themselves **and** changing places with one another **by** diffusion, **as atoms now do and doubtless** have always done when free in space.

If now **we think** of the new made earth in that state, simply **manifesting the law of** repulsion, **its atoms all spread out so as to** be very nearly transparent, **as they certainly** must have been at the first, **there will come to**

our minds the most fitting descriptive words that have ever been written, and these were written thousands of years ago, (Gen. 1:2,)
"And the earth was without form and void."

Yes, and not the earth only, but the material universe entire, as it first emanated from its Creator, invisible to the eyes of men.

I use the words fluids and solids in contrast with each other, so that the two words, fluids and solids, may include every atom of matter in the whole physical world with the ether beyond the skies. The two words relate to matter in exactly opposite conditions and in all possible measures of differences, from the least to the greatest.

Matter in a solid state is always visible and capable of being examined by our senses, always has some cohesion of atoms, and is capable of being acted upon by gravitation and many other laws of coherent matter. But in a fluid state, free from the law of cohesion, we find it manifesting only the opposite; that is, the law of repulsion of all its atoms. Every atom repels every other atom, so that the mass, in the infinity of its numbers, spreads abroad as the fluids of the air are now doing. In this condition all atoms are out of sight, because each one is too small to be seen; but when these same atoms are combined and brought under the law of cohesion, and any two or more of them are chemically united and made one—as, for example, oxygen and hydrogen gas, each one invisible by itself, but when the two are joined by electricity or heat, the product is water, a plainly visible liquid—I do not say fluid, for, by our definition of fluids and solids, water and all liquids are on the side with solids. Some cohesion is manifested in its formation of drops, which is not discoverable in fluids or atoms free in space. In this state, the fluid, repulsion of atoms is the law manifested; in the other cohesion of atoms is the law manifested. The one force makes things visible and many atoms to occupy a small space, in the other matter is invisible and many atoms spread themselves out over a very large space. So it is evident that no microscope can ever show to us an isolated atom of matter. We class water and all other liquids with solids because they are visible and have cohesion in a slight degree. Air and all the gases of every kind, however many there may be, while free in space, the light ether in the skies in which the stars are seen, electricity, magnetism, heat, light and whatever in matter is either matter, or a property or a force manifested in matter and known to move in it as a force without being organized in it as a living thing, we will regard as a fluid.

The practical distinction thus made in all the material things in the whole world is between the seen and the unseen.

The seen things are solids, the unseen are fluids. The heaviest of solids, as gold, may be made volatile by heat, and we often see it in a semi-fluid state giving a golden hue to the smoke that rises skyward from the tall chimney at the mint where gold is fused and liquified for manufacture and coinage.

Electricity has long been called a fluid, and there is no reason for withholding the name from other occult forces exclusive of life and spirit. Let material elements in invisible form be fluids if we speak of them as things, and the same elements when in seen things be solids, and our definition will be easily understood and applied to all material existences as belonging, at the time we are speaking of them, to one or the other of these two classes—

"Seen and Unseen."

The material world, as now understood, by itself consists of many kinds of matter, seventy or more, the exact number not yet known. All these simple kinds of matter are capable of existence and can be found in space free from cohesion, and in that state we can think of them as a vast expanse of misty matter, enough for a world it may be, but without objective form, or gravitation, or manifested, orbital, or axial motions.

But a change came, and art-like a visible world appeared within the invisible; objective form, **cohesion and** gravitation, **orbital and** axial motions, and **numerous other laws** of matter were manifested; and still the law of repulsion continues its manifestations as it did from the beginning and as now seen **in the air.**

The aggregate work **of repulsion is** seen **now in all existing space not taken up** with **solids, and the aggregate work of cohesion** in the world is **seen in** all the solids thus **far made.** To **the eye of** reason the latter must **have come in time** relations after the former.

There is a likeness to this truth in **the** relation of letters to the words in our printed **language.** A few letters (26) are the elements out of which **all the words are** made. **Each letter had an existence before it** had a **place in** any word in which **it is** now found. And we do not think of a dictionary with its **many** thousands **of words as** coming into existence **otherwise** than by collection, arrangements and contribution of letters from the alphabet. **First** the mass of letters, **then** the words, **sentences** and discourses to be put in due form for printing. So in like manner we think of all solids as made of atoms of matter selected from pre-existing matter in a fluid state, but now assembled, arranged and combined so as to cohere together in the beautiful forms we see in greater numbers, thousands of times more in number than the words of the largest dictionary unabridged. To think of one such object as existing before the atoms of which it is made would be to break away from logical thinking, and to bow a leave-taking from our own common sense. Reason stands on the ample evidence that the genesis of every visible thing, and therefore of all the world, was in fluid atoms too small to be seen by the human eye, even with the microscope, and when so crowded as to be faintly visible in places it was a nebulous cloud, "without form and void," incapable in that state of acting conformably to the law of gravitation or of performing any of the distinctive functions of a solid body.

The earth in that condition would manifest supremely the law of repulsion, while all the other laws of matter would for the time being be hidden from our view. We do not imagine they were not in existence, only they could not be manifested to outside observers. It is true that gravitation is discoverable in the air and in gases, but the air is a compound fluid and presumably has some cohesion. It is not entirely invisible for its blue gives us the sky over our heads. There is a strong probability that the fluid ether beyond the sky has no cohesion, and is therefore invisible and the law of repulsion alone is there manifested, and that light is not there obstructed by any atmospheric color.

Notice now that we can see no reason in science or in law why matter might not have remained in that state of repulsion of atoms unchangeably forever, as it was at the creation, an unorganized quantity of material, and there left for eternity. So far as reason is concerned it says nothing against it. But the Creator of the universe had not so intended. He started what He had made to become visible on a great career of changes not yet, if ever, to be completed. The Divine word to the world as a material creation was that it should take up its work and not stay one moment in one state, place and condition; and it did not, but is still progressing onward in its system of orderly changes. But let us think a moment of that marvelous condition of a world all afloat in atoms too small to be seen, some of them to be made into light, and what microscope is there that can show to the eye of man one isolated atom of light? Only the Creator, we believe, has ever seen an ultimate atom of matter. Hence we can never know any difference in the atoms of different substances until, in the laboratory of nature, or art they are brought together, each after its own kind, in sufficient quantities to be appreciable. No single atom ever reflects light or produces any impression upon the most delicate of our sense organs. Yet in such infinitesimal atoms did God create the "heaven and the earth." From this new heaven and earth, in such a state, visible things were eventually made to come forth; and we now see uncounted millions of objects about us free from the manifestation of repulsion and obedient to the law of cohesion.

The field of repulsion is still as vast as it was at the beginning, but there is now a comparatively small field within it in which the law of cohesion is exhibiting in contrast a wonderful world of visible things, and the two laws are now co-acting harmoniously together, but in exact contrast. Reason asks whence came this transference of so many of the atoms of matter and yet not of all of them? Why did not the law or force of cohesion which holds some of all kinds of atoms together in solids, a law which is confessedly everywhere present with power to act, why did it not make a complete victory over repulsion and so hold all the atoms of matter together in solids?

Transforming them from fluidity to solids, or even to one solid mass and nothing more. If cohesion among atoms had been a spontaneity, an inheritance of force in the atoms themselves, such a result would be our reasonable expectation.

But the law of cohesion that has part in all the solids in the world and preserves their integrity, giving to us all the variety and beauty there is in things seen, that law was not a spontaneity. If by any chance thought of ours we might imagine atoms of matter in long time becoming in some way magnetized so as to stick together of themselves, there would be no reason why all atoms should not go right on in like manner accreting together until all should become one mineral mass, an unspeakably worthless thing, and nothing more.

We read of the creation, that "the morning stars sang together and all the sons of God shouted for joy," (Job. 38: 7,) and we may be very certain that the unfolding plans of God, the Father, were seen from above before such thrills of admiration vibrated down upon the work from its high witnesses in heaven. But our question remains—Why did not the force of cohesion take in all the matter of which it did take some? Science has no answer. Philosophy hints no solution. We can see no reason in the laws themselves, and we have not advanced enough in world reading to find an answer. So we must look upwards to the Divine Creator's will. There we find the adequate and ultimate cause of all causes. As our minds are constituted, it is unavoidable that we turn to the personal being who knows, when no other cause can be given, as in this case. We find the law of cohesion acting within certain limitations, just the limitations Infinite beneficence would advise, and we believe God decreed those limitations; but no man can tell why some atoms were taken and some were left. As we can see no reason beforehand, but Our Father's own will, why He made the world, so the adjustments of all the laws of nature, one with another, takes us back to the same fountain of causes.

The Divine beneficence, His love of moral beings, the Fatherhood of God to angels and men, is becoming plainer and plainer as the world's career is better known and the use of its changes better understood. The law of repulsion as first seen was a marvelous display of Divine Power, but it did not then show any moral quality or any good will to men, or that it was to be for the use of men. But now it has an exalted place of usefulness in the world. It has now a moral work, a work of beneficence not exceeded by any other law of physical nature. If we think of what it now does in keeping the air fit for us to breathe, in keeping it in a fit condition to bear the light to our open eyes, in a fit condition for the bright shining orbs of distant worlds to be seen by us, and with all in a fit condition to make life real and joyous and hopeful; whoever will consider the contrast between pure air and malaria, and then behold all the indications of the Divine plan to improve the atmosphere of our world by all the geological changes He appointed for it from the first, will not be wanting in proofs of the beneficence of the Divine Will. All advances in science and religion show this. Compared with the very first this is now a new earth and heaven, and the old is ever vanishing away to give place to the new. We feel that our Heavenly Father intended good results, and provided for them by an ascending scale of creative progress into the future of the world to come. This is our abiding confidence in our Creator Father. It is quite impossible for us who live in a Christian land to feel that the will of God is not beneficent and the safest guide to us for our own well being. Whatever we may fear from our own ill deservings, we do not fear any injustice from the Creator Almighty—"Our Father in Heaven." No other court of final appeal can be opened to us, and no other could compare with this in "**Wisdom, Holiness, Justice, Goodness and Truth.**" The will of Him who is the "King **Eternal, Immortal,** Invisible—the only wise God"— holds the scepter of Righteousness and **Good** Will to men.

It is rather a boast **of science to** explore all known things to their original **elements or sources, to a point** where we can know no more of them at present. And such a vanishing point of human knowledge is always **present in the** final **analysis of any** created thing, when **we must needs refer to** the Divine Will **and stand upon the Omni-**present line **that distinguishes the created** thing from its **Creator—God.**

As we now understand the known things **of the creation of the world, as we** now read the world, **the Supreme Act of Original Creation** included **nothing in itself to be** seen **of men, and** nothing **in itself** known to men.

No one atom of matter in all the universe,

furnished as it now is with atoms made visible in the heaven and the earth, was at first made large enough to be seen of men. And this plan of the Creator's work has never changed. It is now as then, first the unseen then the seen.

"No man hath seen God at any time. The only Begotten Son, which is in the bosom of the Father, he hath declared him."—John 1:18.

All life is from the unseen, and all its normal physical works begin in the use of atoms in an unseen manner; in the use of atoms in such a manner it makes for itself bodies, the seen from the unseen.

We may marvel at such a plan and wonder if God could make a world out of such unstable things, and so great a world without being seen in doing it. But God's ways not as our ways and His thoughts as our thoughts, and His works are not performed as our works are. In World Reading our eyes must look patiently upon the things He has made for us to look upon in the "heaven and in the earth"—seen and unseen.

Behold the witnesses for God! The sun by day leads the train and the moon and stars by night, forever singing as they shine, the hand that

> "Made Us Is Divine."

Truly the heavens declare the glory of God and the firmament showeth His handiwork. Day unto day uttereth speech, and night unto night showeth knowledge. There is no speech nor language where their voice is not heard. Their line is gone out through all the earth, and their words to the end of the world. In them hath He set a tabernacle for the Sun, which is as a bridegroom coming out of his chamber, and rejoiceth as a strong man to run a race. His going forth is from the end of the heaven, and his circuit unto the ends of it, and there is nothing hid from the heat thereof. The law of the Lord is perfect, converting the soul. The testimony of the Lord is sure, making wise the simple. The statutes of the Lord are right, rejoicing the heart. The commandment of the Lord is pure, enlightening the eyes. The fear of the Lord is clean, enduring forever. The judgments of the Lord are true and righteous altogether. More to be desired are they than gold, yea than much fine gold. Sweeter also than honey and the honeycomb. Moreover, by them is thy servant warned, and in keeping of them there is great reward. Who can understand his errors? Cleanse thou me from secret faults. Keep back thy servant also from presumptuous sins; let them not have dominion over me; then shall I be upright and I shall be innocent from the great transgression. Let the words of my mouth and the meditation of my heart be acceptable in thy sight, "O Lord, My Strength and My Redeemer."—Ps. 19.

"And darkness was upon the face of the deep."

—GENESIS, 1:2.

SOLIDS AND FLUIDS.

CHAPTER II.

We have defined the words, fluids and solids; names of all the matter in the world in opposite conditions of atoms and revealing to us the opposite laws, repulsion and cohesion.

As long as the world consisted of atoms, all in a state of repulsion of one another, no human conception of a solid earth coming out of them could reasonably be formed. Hence the outcome of a visible world in the midst of those created atoms, "without form and void," was a transformation, on its first appearance, truly wonderful beyond expression. As things are now manifested around us the number of atoms held together in solids, the visible world, gains our first attention. And we are liable to think of the invisible world as a place pretty far away and not as a place into which we are born, and in which we are still living, though it be at the lower border of it where it broods on the visible.

We are not told in simple words in what way or by what means the earth, "without form and void," was made ready to evolve the visible world out of its midst, or so to divide its atoms that some of them should be made to evolve from the invisible to the visible state and thus to manifest the law of cohesion, while others remained as they were, spread abroad to the outer boundaries of creation as far as the law of repulsion has dominion. But we are furnished with the most graphic picture ever written of what the world looked like when that change was in progress. "And darkness was upon the face of the deep." Gen. 1 : 2. This, like the first view of the earth after its creation, was taken by an outside observation. The darkness was seen objectively as a visible

Solids and Fluids.

thing, and thus cohesion was manifested as a law acting upon material atoms in solids. We must know, however, that cohesion acts only between atoms at an insensible distance apart and never directly upon matter in a state of repulsion of atoms. Cohesion does not collect atoms; it holds them together when they touch each other; hence we do not mean to say in any case that cohesion alone makes solids, but that solids always do manifest that law to us as a constant law of their existence.

It is reasonable for us therefore to ask how the atoms so situated in space became disposed to a simultaneous act of self assembling in readiness to cohere? How were they removed from their first situation abroad and apart and so drawn together as to become visible, becoming obedient to a new law and to many new laws besides the law of cohesion? The atoms now cohering in the earth and all the solids of the same must have spread out in a state of repulsion millions of miles around and away from any common centre. The question is, who gave so many of them a rallying impulse, a simultaneous mobility towards a common centre? In a general way they moved up to each other and all towards a common centre. The existence of the visible earth is proof that something of that kind has taken place; atoms did come together, for here they are under the law of cohesion, many of them solid rocks, and every one of them has the true character of a transformation from a fluid state. Whatever may have been the distance apart of these atoms in the atomic world before they were collected, at the time appointed they arrived at the places where we now find them in this small central part of the first created atomic world. We here notice a well-known and universal law of matter, which is, that motion with compression of atoms always produces heat in proportion to the rapidity of motion and intensity of pressure combined. We judge therefore that the motion and compression of atoms concerned in this first stage of the world evolution, by which the solids came forth, must have produced a volume of heat of such intensity as to stagger arithmetical calculations.

Heat by chemical action was, of course, one of the forces in this compression, as well as electricity; but that does nothing to solve the question, or to tell how the atoms were made ready for that special, electrical and chemical action, either alone or with other forces.

The compression of matter by whatever means from a volume so immense as the earth was in its nebulous form, and is now in its unseen part, to a sphere so small as 8000 miles in diameter, must have produced an enormous amount of heat in the compressed materials; while at the same time the outlying and surrounding space would be so rarefied by the matter withdrawn from it as to occasion a high degree of cold in all the space so rarefied. The compression of atoms would generate fervent heat and the rarefaction of the outlying atoms from which they were taken the most intense cold. So we may, for the time, think of a fiery centre all aglow with consuming heat, inclosed in a hollow sphere of vaporous fluid of intensest cold. The two states of matter, hot and cold, are placed in the strongest contrast and their battle ground is now between them.

If we stop here we shall not get the world's true appearance as it must have been at that time. A glowing ball of fire was not what an outside observer at a distance would have seen, for we find that the elements of the solids of the earth are not all capable of being solidified by heat alone. Some of them cannot be so solidified. Water, the largest of all the external solids, cannot, though heat is generated in its production by the union of the gases in the chemical and electrical fire that forms it; when thus formed into water it is by heat turned into steam, and wafted by heat force into the cold air surrounding it, where it becomes a dense cloud of vapor and cooling returns to water and ice. When we think of all the liquids, with their respective properties, as carbon and other materials that heat would turn into smoke and steam to be condensed on reaching the outside cold circle above, yet somewhat nearer the fiery mass than the circle of extreme cold, we shall see at once that it was not the fiery ball that an outside observer would see far away from without, but rather the darkness of the steam and smoke inclosing the globe of fire within it. This outside wrapper that the consumption of gases must have produced could have been nothing else than a globe of darkness. When a great city is on fire it is not the fire that is seen afar off, but the smoke. When Abraham looked away upon the burning Sodom and Gomorrah, the cities of the plain, "Lo, the smoke of the country went up as a furnace," (Gen. 19 : 28.)

The greater the fire the greater the darkness to a distant outside observer must be, until the fuel becomes incandescent, for however high the flames may mount up the smoke keeps always above it with its darkness. Combustion is a process of intense chemical action in which two or more kinds of elements must undergo extreme changes. If we think of an electric fire 8,000 miles in diameter, over 25,000 miles in circumference, all aglow under the great open arch of creation, and fed by the inflow of all the chemical atoms that became the solids of the earth, including liquids, we shall find it impossible to exaggerate the quantity of smoke that rose to the rarefied ether, to the cold above it around the whole circle of the globe.

Let us call the earth as it then was, "A Deep," and then say, "And darkness was upon the face of the deep," (Gen. 1:2)— A deep of fire around which was an envelope of smoke, within which the elemental fire of creation was making ready the materials to come forth in due time as the original solids of the earth at its own natural center of the world. Chemical transformations are pre-eminently like new creations. No man can forecast what the product will be from any new combination of elements chemically united. We have learned that carbon and oxygen so uniting produce fire during the process of uniting and then leave a resultant that is counter fire. And though to outward appearances the carbon is gone, it is not. It is simply transformed into a gaseous state and combined with the oxygen that consumed it. And though the change is so inconceivably great, nothing is lost; and presumably these changes will continue to produce surprising transformations forever, and that not one atom will be destroyed thereby. Neither fire nor anything else ever destroy the atoms of matter, but only set them free to form new combinations or to go again under the law of repulsion and diffusion. All combinations are formed by definite laws, and many of them in definite proportions of atoms also. Thus we see reasons for an enormous heat in the chemical processes of the fluids brought together in making their endless adjustments. But as fast as adjustments were reached in the formation of compounds, rocks, metals and water, a comparative state of quietude must have ensued.

How long the hot world was kept busy with its chemical adjustments with rock, metals, salts, alkalies, acids, carbon and lime before the removal of its outside darkness, we cannot tell. Internal chemical action in all the elements of its mineral formation, keeping up heat, steam and smoke in opposition to the ethereal cold beyond it, would indicate a condition that might be so balanced as to continue for long ages of time. The Bible gives us no hint upon this question. We are left with full liberty to take all the time needed. But it must have been an exceedingly long time before all the processes of nature included in the formation of the complete list of mineral solids now known, together with all the changes of place and state in the elements that could be affected as well without the direct rays of the sun as with them, were fully accomplished. Evidently it may have extended through millions of years. It must have continued until the world was shaped up to a great extent and its crust became cool enough in places to allow carbon to be taken up in vegetable organisms, and lime to be worked over and used by animal lives for the frame work of their bodies, that is shells. And until much of the condensed steam upon it was reduced to the form of water. And not only so, but an enormous quantity of water. If a fraction of the water now on the earth were turned into steam at the earth's surface, an envelope of fog would again cut off the direct rays of the sun and darkness would again be on the earth during its continuance, and yet, possibly, without stopping in a large degree some of the processes of nature.

I emphasize my remark that much may have been done in the world without the direct rays of the sun, and before the sun could have been clearly seen from its surface, because it is reasonable in itself and accordant with the report given in Genesis. "God said let there be light and there was light," evidently before the firmanent was completed and while the skyward region was in a state of mixture of light and darkness as we now have in foggy mornings. Fogs in England sometimes obscure for days the direct rays of the sun over their well kept and beautiful fields and gardens. Probably the sun's rays did not touch the solid parts of the earth so as to reveal its own bright form in the heavens, as seen from the earth for a long time after it was lighting the earth sufficiently for some purposes. Perhaps not until a comparatively late period. Certainly not until the granite and other primary rocks had been formed and cooled down in part, then broken up again and again, and seethed and boiled in the liquid floods, and still cooling in greater quantities until rocks and mountains and volcanoes began to make a frame work over the fiery deep and amid the immensity of prevailing waters, before the fog could have cleared away. It may have been that at any time during long ages, if need be, an outside observer looking towards the earth would see but a globe of darkness, for we must not forget that this view was objective and that the observer's standpoint was outside of the earth until a firmament was made.

"God said let there be a firmament in the midst of the waters, and let it divide the waters from the waters." Gen. 1 : 6. Now the observer's standpoint must be entirely changed. He must now be down upon the solids of the earth, which are a very small part of its whole magnitude, and the firmanent must be over him. And thus the materials of the whole world throughout all of its original space, including the firmament, all that was included in the "beginning when God created the heaven and the earth," is clearly separated into two mineral parts—the

SOLIDS AND FLUIDS.

Science teaches that all that is known as matter in the world may be conveniently divided into three classes, and that each one of these classes may be called a kingdom. The first, which is the mineral kingdom, then the vegetable and animal kingdoms. And now where do we place the air in which all the fluids, the gases and extended ether by which the light comes to us from the sun and the moon and the stars, where shall we place all the matter that exists in a fluid state? Not in the animal kingdom certainly, for animals have form and organs of life by which they may be known separately, even microscopic lives may be known separately. The air in its nature is not animal and does not belong to the animal kingdom. Is the air then a vegetable? Well, vegetables have form and organs of life and a place to stay while they grow, and where they may be found to-day and to-morrow. "But the wind bloweth where it listeth and we hear the sound thereof, but cannot tell whence it cometh and whither it goeth." This is not a vegetable; and now we are left alone in the mineral kingdom. Each of the others has failed us. If we cannot get gaseous fluids, the air and like matter in here, it will be left out alone with no class to receive it. But it is not left out. The essential elements of matter in the air and of all fluids are mineral elements. In every human breath there is some carbonic acid gas, some carbon. And the diamond, among the hardest of minerals and the most brilliant of gems, is nearly all carbon. Reduce the diamond to invisible atoms and it will still be mineral. In our breaths the atoms of carbon are fluid, or free in space and in a state of repulsion, while in the diamond like atoms are held in a state of cohesion in the closest of contact, like atoms, indeed, but changed in their relations to one another from a state of repulsion to a state of cohesion. This change does not remove them from one and the same kingdom. Air and all fluids, as we have defined fluids, belong to the mineral kingdom, in distinction to the other two kindgoms, animal and vegetable. This should be understood strictly as pertaining to its essential atoms in the invisible fluid state. We would not call a visible drop of water a mineral, nor a gust of wind a mineral. But we must and do class the elements of these things in the mineral kingdom, because their essential atoms are mineral and readily distinguishable from organized matter in either animal or vegetable. All unorganized matter is mineral.

The original creation revealed only the mineral kingdom in a fluid state and of atoms singly too small to be seen of men. It is well to keep this in mind always in considering the history of the elements through their many transformations before their present appearance in visible things around us. By the first formation of solids the mineral kingdom was divided into two parts as unlike each other as opposite states of matter can be, and still that dividing process was only the beginning of changes in both parts of the kingdom. As to solids, themselves, but very few if any of them can now be shown to be in the exact conditions of their original formation. As to the rocks, they have been broken up, cast out of volcanoes, tumbled about and mashed in pieces and ground to powder; reformed and broken up again and ground and washed and mixed, made plastic and again hardened. Some conglomerated, and by the mechanical forces of nature thrown into the lodgments of the earth where we now find them. Some in the everlasting hills, and some beneath the bottom of the seas. All have been fire worked and water worked, and very many indeed have been life worked into the soils and chemicals of the earth, and into sediments beneath its waters, and into vegetable and animal organisms. All the mechanical and all the electrical and all the life forces of this world are ever active in preparing matter for new conditions and uses, new combination and appearances, so that creation itself in its grand career of progress is a daily promiser of a new heaven and a new earth. Geology teaches us plainly that long ages before man appeared in the world life was here in great power in both vetetable and animal forms. There were vegetable growths of marvelous dimensions and in great varieties, and animals great and small, from the megatherium and other monsters down to minute forms, living things of microscopic dimensions. Fossils of many kinds, both flora and fauna, are found in the earth's crusts after the first. So prolific in plant and tree growths was the earth long ages ago, as to support the animals of that time and leave a residuum sufficient for the coal beds we are now mining and distributing for the use of man. Also, on the animal side, the mere bones and shells of past generations occupy no small place among the solids of the earth, so obviously did lower lives work in ages past and left the results of their labors in a better prepared world for the use of man.

Carbon was not solidified by heat alone, neither by cold; but it required life, vegetable and animal, to solidify it. And so in respect to the elements of chalk-beds and lime-stone and coral-reefs; their elements were operated upon by life-agencies, animal life, and thus reduced to solids and removed from the atmosphere in such quantities as to make an atmosphere of use to higher orders of beings. The fossils of the earth's crust are no very small part of its solids, and many of them must have been entombed long before the creation of man. Let all the carbon and lime now in solids as fossil remains be turned again into a gaseous form, and the air would be, the world over, unfit for human beings as we are now constituted. The truth of the early introduction of life into visible forms seems to give a reason for the words following: "And the spirit of God moved upon the face of the waters." (Gen. 1;2.) We notice that the largest part of the earth's surface is even now liquid—water. There is something very significant in the Bible names given to the world in its different states after its creation, while on its way of readiness for man. First, It was named broadly with its own proper name: In the beginning God created the "heaven and the earth." Second, When it began to be objectively visible to a very slight extent, its proper name is repeated and a descriptive clause subjoined: "And the earth was without form and void." Third, It is called the "Deep," and the descriptive word "darkness" is subjoined: "And darkness was upon the face of the deep." Fourth, It is called waters, as God again acted upon it: "And the spirit of God moved upon the face of the waters." It is evident that the author of such descriptive words was well instructed about the genesis of the world and the stages of its progressive career. But it is equally evident that he did not intend to give any detailed account of it. We find that every word that bears upon the creation is pointing directly and with emphasis to its Creator. The object was to tell *who* made the world and not *how* He did it, any further than a few brief signs would help to settle the fact that God made it in its beginning and all the way after it. He gives the key to the study of its elements, and names the appearances of its earlier transformations, and then leads on with directness and force to Theology and Religion. "And the spirit of God moved upon the face of the waters." This implies a life-giving presence of God over the elements thus described, and we presume that the vegetable and animal lives introduced at that time were not, any of them, to come up to observation in review as a part of the instruction to be given by revelation respecting the doctrines of Theology and Religion. The distinct mention that God did act upon the waters and moved upon them, before the sun is mentioned as having been seen from man's standpoint on the solid earth, makes it probable that He supplied all the kinds of life that were suited to that time, and that all the laws of life possible at that time were duly inaugurated and continue in force, wherever matter is conditioned to receive them, until this day. It would be hard to show that any law of nature has ever been repealed. As the temperature and food required by certain kinds of life superabounded long ages before the world was ready for man's use, we have no reason to doubt that a life grant was Divinely given to all creatures, great and small, capable of exercising the functions of life at that time.

It is always reasonable to have regard to the intentions of an author in explaining the words he sets before us. Why did the author of the first chapter of the Bible refer to the creation of the world except to say in the most positive manner that all this, in all the views that can be taken of it and in all that it can include, was the work of God? and to emphasize it strongly as a fact by declaring that he did it in such a way as to show a series of changes in its progress, and to include all that can be learned by human observation now or at any time? First, God created it at the beginning. He was its author when it was in material atoms; was "without form and void." After that it became enveloped in darkness: "Darkness was upon the face of the deep," when cohesion took place and the solids were made, including the waters. After the waters, life was introduced in organisms, "the spirit of God moved upon the waters." life was given to the visible part of the world. Light came by God's commandment. He made the firmament, and night and day became an established fact. He appointed seas and furnished the water, and the air and the land with all the varieties of Life-forms that preceded the introduction of man; and in His own time he made man in His own image. "Let us make man in our image." "So God created man in His own image, in the image of God created he him, male and female created he them."

This likeness included the idea of instructing men by the Divine example, the enforcement of Divine precepts by Divine examples. This one principle started in the first chapter of the Bible and runs through the whole book. "Be ye holy," says God to us, "for I am holy." "Be ye followers of God as dear children," implying a natural affection that should be a life joy in the hearts of men loving God as their "Father in heaven." "Put ye on the Lord Jesus." I see no reason for the mention of a six days which are named with such exactness of description: "And the evening and the morning were the first day," etc., but to place God before us working six days and resting on the seventh, and thus, by his own example, made the Sabbath to follow the six days of labor just as he requires us to keep it. He made it to follow the sixth day of labor to us as we count time, and He applied this measure of time to himself figuratively—the only possible way of its applicaton by finite minds—to bring His own example before us in regard to the Sabbath day, and to show that it is sanctified and holy, ordained of

God for the use of man. The language is figurative as applied to the works of God, but it is literal as it stands in connection with the decalogue and all other Scripture teaching on the subject of the Sabbath day. We should hesitate to adopt any view of the six days that would take them out of harmony with Bible teaching on the subject of the Sabbath day. In this matter, on the human side these days must be construed literally for our instruction, to give us the measure of time intended for our weekly use, in work or rest; and figuratively, to give us the condescending example of God in respect to His work and rest in the works of creation. In the second chapter of this book, fourth verse, in which the Sabbath is not concerned, the time of creation is designated indefinitely by a mere allusion to it as a fact: "In the day that the Lord God made the earth and the heavens." (Gen. 2:4.) This shows that "day" as we count days, is not to be taken as a time measure of the act of God in the creation. A moment's careful reflection will show us that there is no way in which we can measure any work of God by time measure as applied to Himself without intermediate agencies. Divine acts are not time acts in the sense of lingering through space with no intermediate agencies. God appoints the time and season for others, but we cannot take these up and apply them to Him or to any of His direct and literal works. We cannot say that God made a mammoth California tree in one moment, or in one hour—a tree that has been growing fifteen hundred years; neither can we say that he was fifteen hundred years in making it. We can say fifteen hundred years have passed since that tree was planted, since the seed from which it grew was placed in the soil. But the question, "When was that tree made?" remains unanswered, because we cannot discover the beginning and end of a Divine act in such a way as to apply any time measure to it before it is in the keeping, as it were, of some intermediate agency put under laws distinguishable from God Himself, although of His own will made, appointed and determined. The tree has been growing in soil, air, moisture and sunshine, and the seed came from its parent tree. So we may follow back through mediate causes as long as we please, and when we get to the end of all answerable questions we shall have failed to learn how long God took to make that tree, or what to include in that act less than the creating of all the world.

Probably no man living knows what to include in the making of the world. Let a young thinker try to think just what he will include in the making of the world, and if he thinks clearly and closely, as he should, he will find an honest answer in three short words, "I don't know." There are no time measures of any kind, either long or short, that can be applied to it as a work of time— a creation that was set in motion and started on the career of successive changes, within limitations, just as long as it shall endure, or is to have any being, and still endowed with elements that are indestructible. To say that it was made in millions of years, and finished 6,000 years ago, cannot be true, and is subject to the same denial that any other literal time statement would be. The world is not now what it was 6,000 years ago, or 6 days ago, strictly speaking. If we choose to fall back in the world's career by definite measures of 6,000 years at a time, we may repeat that time measure as long as we can count it, and then leave the question as far from answer as ever, and no man able to tell what he includes in the world's creation. Therefore, there is no scientific or provable time, known or unknown, when the work of the creation began, or when it was or will be finished. Any expression more than the first verse of the Bible contains must of necessity be figurative. The Bible statement is positive and true: "In the beginning God created the heaven and the earth." That is literal. The institution of the Sabbath is also a literal and positive fact. Man is required to so observe time and labor that every seventh day shall be Sabbath time. The Bible says nothing about the time taken for the creation except in connection with the Sabbath day and to show that God made that distinction in the use of the days, and made it honorable for man to observe it in all time by his own example, which was of necessity a figurative illustration. In no other way is the work of creation referred to as a labor finished, but to emphasize the rest time that God has made and keeps in reserve for His people. (Heb. 4 : 4-9.) "For He spake in a certain place of the seventh day on this wise. And God did rest the seventh day from all His work." "There remains therefore a rest to the people of God." We conclude therefore that all the truths intended to be taught from the first chapter of the Bible are plain so far as Theology and Religion are concerned. That the word "day" for man's use is literal, but not limited to a literal sense as applied to the Creator's acts in making the heaven and the earth : "In the day that the Lord God created them."

If we consider that it is the world itself, and mainly the solid part of it, that makes the days, the first day and all that have followed it, it will be obvious that days are used in a figurative sense when applied to anything that was previously made or done. The world makes days by its revolution on its axis successively every twenty-four hours, or it makes twenty-four hours in one day. But it did not make either days or hours before it had an existence or itself was made in the sense of being and moving in conformity to gravitation, momentum and other laws. It is inconceivable to us how time was measured before there was any revolving world to measure it. All our time measures are known by the world's daily revolution on its axis, and we cannot say that the world revolved before it was made. Another step in our existence may take us another step in knowledge, but these are our limitations now as to the time of creation.

The Bible does not speak of day until it

was visibly made by the revolution of the earth upon its axis: "God divided the light from the darkness," (for the first day and for all the days ever to be made by the revolution of the earth on its axis) "And God called the light day and the darkness He called night. And the evening and the morning were the first day." Gen. 1: 4, 5.

It is often said that the Bible was not given to teach science. But there is a science of Theology and Religion, and this the Bible teaches. Science is simply knowledge obtained by observations and experiments which may be repeated by others who are qualified to repeat the experiments and to make correctly the observations. All truths so obtained in regard to any subject constitute the science of that subject, as the science of Astronomy is what is known of astronomy by agreeing observations of many, and is correctly taught to others as the science of astronomy. The Bible teaches Theology and Religion, and it teaches that subject in a strictly scientific way. It points to facts to be considered by the observations of competent men. It asserts the principles and characteristics of moral and spiritual character, and it points to experiments and works done to prove the truth of all its doctrines. Experiments underlie all its requirements. There is a constant call for men to exercise themselves in experimental proofs of all the doctrines the Bible sets before them as the pillars of truth. Its first words teach the true doctrine of one God only, by pointing to the creation of the world and all things that are in it, and can be seen from it, so that nothing exists upon which any claims of another god can be placed. The great truth that one being made it all and all created things known to men settles the question by the exclusion of all other gods, and this is a scientific method, bringing before us a world which we are to examine for ourselves, simply noting that in its first appearance it was not more than thin nebula, "without form and void;" then the stages through which it passed in preparation for the use of man, a work of intelligent design, variety and magnitude. This one truth of creation by one present Creator, the material world, as an example of His work, brought under our own observation as we now see it, together with the views of what it has been in some other stages of its career, entitles the Bible to be a true text-book of the Theology and Religion to be taught to men. One God is the first doctrine of true theology, and the Bible teaches this doctrine without prejudice to the mode of His own being, or to the methods of His foreordained plan of human redemption by Christ, the Son of God and of man.

Another true doctrine is the Divine ordination of the Sabbath day, coming in at the close of the six days of labor and commended by His own example as a rest day and a holy day, founded on the experimental testing of God for its right. Certainly such a method of teaching by example, founded on experimental proof before giving to men the precept, is truly scientific. If we take up any other doctrine of the Bible, we find that it presents to us, in the same reasonable way, proper grounds for our investigation before acceptance. No book in the world calls us to closer observations, more careful experiments, or clearer illustrations. "By their fruits ye shall know them." "Whatsoever a man soweth, that shall he reap." "If any man will do His will he shall know of the doctrine whether it be of God, or whether I speak of myself." Nothing is more scientific than such experimental methods—practical tests of truth as these—the Divine works as an open book always before us, with its testimonies for our examination. And "Scripture given by inspiration of God, is open for our inspection and information, as well as for reproof, for correction, for instruction in righteousness, that the man of God may be perfect, thoroughly furnished unto all good works." 2 Tim. 3 : 16, 17. It is thus made plain that the purpose of revelation is to help us in our observations and experiments, so that all who strive to find the truth may find it. In nature we find no power visible in itself, or life visible in itself. When power, force or life are manifested in matter they can be differentiated from it, from all visible things. Hence the outgoing of our faith to the infinite Omnipresent God is not unreasonable nor unscientific. Invisibility is a necessity of Omnipresence; hence the man of God in all ages, speaking to his Father in heaven, as a present person, can say with reverence and a holy unction:

"Whither shall I go from Thy spirit? Or whither shall I flee from Thy presence? If I ascend up into heaven, Thou art there. If I make my bed in hell, behold Thou art there. If I take the wings of the morning and dwell in the uttermost part of the sea, even there shall Thy hand lead me, and Thy right hand shall hold me. If I say surely the darkness shall cover me, even the night shall be light about me. Yea, the darkness hideth not from Thee, but the night shineth as the day, the darkness and the light are both alike to Thee." (Ps. 139 : 7-12)

"And God said, Let the earth bring forth grass, the herb yielding seed, and the fruit tree yielding fruit after his kind, whose seed is in itself, upon the earth; and it was so."

—GENESIS, 1:11.

LIFE AND COUNTER LIFE.

CHAPTER III.

We have considered matter in its opposite states, seen and unseen, solids and fluids. We believe the unseen was the condition of all the materials of the world and of the universe: "In the beginning when God created the heaven and the earth." Out of that condition the atoms required for solids were taken by a force that produced a gaseous conflagration, and, of consequence, an overspreading cloud of smoke in all directions around the formative globe-mass of cohering matter. This darkness manifested the law of cohesion, and eventually there came into view the solid globe now under our feet. The aggregate of solids, as weighed in the world balances at that stage of creation, were, we presume, the same as now.

From that time the material world has consisted of these two parts in exactly opposite conditions of matter, the unseen including all the fluids wherever they are, and the seen including all the solids wherever they are. We might pause here to look at the new made solids, wonderful in magnitude and in workmanship, endless in variety—the great floods of water, the high mountains and deep valleys, the rocks, metals, earths and formative solutions of mineral atoms in process of crystallization, crystals and gems—but our plan requires us to notice, in a general way, a phenomenon that occurred in time long before many of the minerals had their places and finish as we now see them. There was another outcome from the invisible part of the world before the manufacture of the most picturesque minerals was concluded. A new kind of force comes out of the unseen world before us and makes itself known here in varied and wonderful kinds of conduct. This new comer is called life. It emerged from the unseen world in the quietest possible manner. In its own nature an invisible force, it greatly surpasses all we had before seen or known in matter by its own peculiar way of using it. It makes atoms of matter visible to us in forms and ways not revealed in cohesion, or in any before known laws of matter—a new phenomenon, and we pause for a while to think of it. It shows itself in numberless and multiplying individualities, shaping for itself, in matter, the greatest variety of forms, sizes, habitats and combinations of parts and members, all made of the two conditions of matter we have been considering as seen and unseen —solids and fluids.

Science says that all matter is either organized or unorganized. Only life can organize matter. Until life came there was no organized matter in the world, and there is none now but that which the individual lives here have organized for themselves. It follows that the organized matter is simply the living bodies of all the distinct living things there are in the world at any one time, including the full number of vegetables and animals.

This new phenomenon of living workers over all the world organizing matter into material plants and animals comes to our view from the unseen, as all the solids came, and it shows to us another unfolded space in the plan of God in the creation of the world—another evolution. We see life as a predetermined, foreordained organizer of so much of the world's materials in fluids and solids as to lift them above the low level of inert matter. At this stage of world reading we see it as a habitation for an endless variety of lives of both animal and vegetable, and we pause to look at the situation given it to manifest itself in visible organisms, the place made ready for it, life's dwelling place in respect to the seen and unseen things, while it exercises itself in material bodies. It may be said to reside here.

Broadly speaking: Just between these two parts of the world, the solids and fluids;

at the top of the solid globe, just on the shell of the world's core and at the bottom of its great ocean of fluid atmosphere that rises into heaven; in this space in every direction all over the world; at the top of this comparatively small globe of solids, with its crust but partially concealing many fiery billows below, as shown by structure, earthquakes and volcanoes, hot springs and geysers, with other evidences of enveloped heat; at the bottom of an atmosphere opening up above us for unknown miles through the blue sky into the infinite space beyond the stars in heaven; in this lowly place, as it were, the footstool of heaven; at the bottom of all that is free in space in all directions, we see the place designed for the homes and the labors, the food and the enjoyments of all the living of every kind, with the camps and battlefields, the graves and monuments of all the dead of every kind. Here are all the throbbing pulses out of the living hearts of men with anxious desires, hopes and fears, wrestling for changes, for higher stations, for better conditions of life. On this one stage of solids are the endless variety of persons and characters coming into view as persons and dropping out of view as persons, but sustained in numbers and variety—a moving panorama throughout all generations. True, some lives, just a few, are organized to soar upward at will high in the air, on wings, for a little while, and some to plunge at will deep below the billows of the sea on mere occasions, but none can stay long or very far from this common breathing place for all the living and resting place for all the dead—the place of contact between the seen and the unseen, the solids and the fluids of the mere dead matter of creation as we know it by our senses.

But more than this: Physical life is never manifested, never organizes itself by use of atoms in either of these two states of matter alone. The two are always joined together in a wonderful manner before there is any phenomenon of life in any matter whatever. The bodies of all life forms are solid, and the work of life in all its motions, whatever it does, is carried on in the use of fluid atoms. Every living thing keeps its own body alive only by its contributions to itself of fluid atoms, largely obtained at times by the conversion of solids into fluid atoms by digestion in its body, and when this process of fluid action ceases, for any reason whatever, physical life ceases in the organism with which it was identified. Hence we see the two states of matter are essential to life itself and are represented in all the tiniest as well as the largest of this world's living forms, in both the vegetable and animal kingdoms.

The foods of every kind of organism must include both kinds of matter. Every living organism must have some food in such form that it can work upon it and accomplish such conversion of it into fluid as its own needs require; something solid, including liquids and solids, from which to extract its needed fluids. Also, the ejections, wastes and exhalations of every life organism will be found to include matter in both the solid and fluid state. The odors of plants are fluids and their shed leaves are solids; their roots draw fluid food from the surrounding soil, and their leaves take in fluids from the surrounding atmosphere. So every tree takes food from above as well as from below, and cannot dispense with either source of its supplies. Such is the relationship of every living thing to matter in its two states—fluids and solids, seen and unseen.

We notice the order of the outcoming things from the unseen part of the world. Solids were the first thing we saw coming out from thence. They came out of the store-house of invisible things, which store-house our Father in heaven has not yet opened visibly to the eyes of men; and now comes life, the second thing that has come forth from the same store-house of unseen things which are kept somewhere in our Heavenly Father's universal kingdom under his control and not yet made visible to men.

We cannot think of life as coming from the solids; it was not given with solids, did not come when they came. Its hiding place is in the fluids, and there is not a physical life in the world that can give up its fluids and not its place in matter at the same time. Life comes and goes in fluid matter, distinct as it is from it, for it has no material properties. It brings nothing to the scales as a counterpoise to the small dust of the balance. We do not imagine that a live elephant placed upon the scales and weighed should he be then and there electrocuted, or yield his life to an electric shock, would weigh either less or more because of that event. Ponderability is not a property of life, neither has life any part in the essential properties of matter as we know it.

The true science of life comes only from the works of life itself. We must see what it does and define it by its works; after that determine what its laws are, when we know sufficiently of its works to do so. This is all that science, simply as science, knows about life; it knows it by its works. We need not try to break the mystery of its being. We know it as a part of the wonderful works of God. We may classify it and study it boldly and carefully, but as there is always in it a kind of Godward mystery we should study it reverently, with open minds and truth-loving hearts.

Probably the word life has a greater range of meanings than any other word. It belongs individually to every organized form in the whole universe. The vivified speck of organized matter that, with flickering heart-beats, begins the battle of existence on wings and expires in the contest of one day, as the ephemera or May flies are said to do, is individualized life, and it ranges up through the whole scale of individual existence. Life is thus used with a universality not given to many, if to any other, words. There is nothing else more multitudinous than life organisms in the world.

Because electricity is universally present and imponderable, and it is always found abundantly in all organized beings, some have said that may be life. But if electricity were life it is very singular that an abundance of it is so fatal everywhere to all life, vegetable and animal. No, electricity is not life any more than heat or light or magnetism is life. Life did not come into solids as electricity came, and it did not come until after electricity came. Electricity came with the first manifestation of solids, but life came in a characteristic manner that belongs to itself alone. It came without visible form, to build visible forms. It came without visible faculties to organize for itself visible faculties. It came with no visible will power and it crowned many things it organized with faculties for adequately showing the character of a free will. It came with no visible eyes to see its own work, but it included organs of sight in most of its animal productions. It came with no visible relations to material things and it has filled the world with visible forms that are related to one another and yet diversified in powers, characters and works and moral attributes revealed as subsisting with, and yet distinct from, the materials in which they reside. No building ever made a builder. No statuary ever made an artist. Life came as the world came, by the word of God. "God said." And that is the reason solids came with electricity, and then life, not as the law of electricity or any other law of matter. Life is an individualizing power and has characteristics that do not belong to any law of matter. It has use for and ability to use matter, as no laws of matter can do without it. Life individualizes itself in fairly reasonable proportions in two opposite sexes, the male and the female. And the increase of numbers of individuals in all kinds of life, vegetable and animal, is dependent on a parentage that includes both sexes. The foundations of religious marriage were started prospectively in this world with the introduction of life. And the higher the life the more sacred and divine is that relationship of which Christ and His Church is the antitype. Eph. 5:

xxxii: "This is a great mystery, but I speak concerning Christ and the Church."

Again we notice that embodied life in both kingdoms and of all kinds, begins its manifestation to us, its very first work, in starting for itself a body, beginning always with the making of a seed in the body of its own natural parent from which it is to descend. This special fact belongs in principle to all animated nature without exception, life from life. There has never been known in historic times any life without parentage, natural descent or the body or seed of any life not commenced in a living relation to a parent of which it has a natural time limit of separation. Only life can generate life, and of all the kinds of life in the world no one can generate either a higher or lower kind than is natural to itself. Sparrows cannot generate eagles, nor eagles sparrows; apples grapes, nor grapes apples. Though the seeds of a tree, vast in numbers, to be counted by thousands, it is still true that every one of them is a separate young life commenced in the tree and shows the first steps taken in embryo to make another tree like the one from which the seed came. And so in all animals multiplying by whatever kind of eggs, or spawn, or dividings, and whatever their number from the same parent. The spawn eggs of some kinds of fish may be counted to a million, it is said, yet every one of them contains the embryo of another animal in the likeness of its parent fish, as seeds do of new trees in the likeness of their parent tree. We notice, also, that the seeds of every tree and the eggs of all animals that are parted from their parent before an independent life is manifested have in a safe casing or shell a little food for the young tree or the young animal to start with and to live upon for a little time whenever the little life germ shall be placed in circumstances to start independently, or on its own account. As an example we are all familiar with the food in a common hen's egg that lasts three weeks under the vivifying influences of incubation, in which time the embryo grows by feeding on the repast of egg food stored up for it for that occasion, as long as it lasts. Then the chick's growth and strength is such that with its little bill it breaks a hole in the shell which held his food for three weeks and was his own little world when he began life and was called an egg; then master chick comes out to see the outside world and to gather food wherever he can find it, in a place where he can use his numerous faculties, eyes, ears, bill, legs, claws and wings, brains and intellectual faculties. If we turn now to the tiniest seed of grass, when it leaves the place of its paternity, it has a small well packed case of food in its tiny, almost microscopic casing, for its first use whenever it shall be placed in circumstances for going on with its enterprise of making another blade of grass like that from which it came, including the production of seeds and casting them forth with life properties and food in them like that with which it started its own career. Thus in endless multiplications and successions all the orders of life are going on to accomplish their work. We see their bodies, their growth and their work while they live. They die, and their bodies cease to be organized matter, they cannot be used as bodies for any other lives, even if used as shelter or food for them, for in this respect parasites must make their own bodies. That is a work the doing of which cannot be shirked or delegated to another, either bond or free, high or low, great or small, each life must grow its own body.

Notice also that life always extends itself by individuals and in no other way. Mollusca may increase as the sands of the sea, and insects swarm as clouds, and fish may shoal in masses and grass may sward the lawn; still a careful analysis will show that all these aggregated numbers of each kind are made up of individuals, and that each individual has only such a body as it has made for itself and such as form its seed or root multiplication; it could have made no other in substantial character. The egg is not like the fish that spawned it, nor the seed like the tree that bore it or the root that branched it; yet the law of descent will keep them both within their proper lines in all their future work. If we think of the unnumbered classes of life forms in the waters and the air and on the land, the preservation of classes is indeed most wonderful. But all seeds hold their secret unseen of men, they hold the plan and character of the material body from which they came, but will not reveal it until given an opportunity similar to that enjoyed by the parent tree. I may hold a mustard seed and a turnip seed in my hand and be unable to tell by sight the one from the other, but when placed in fertile soil, smiling sunshine and ample moisture they will open their respective plans with all the cautions of invisible growth; but eventually, faithful to their parentage, a true likeness of the plant that gave them respectively their being comes forth.

The microscope has been called into service to discover the secrets of life in its starting, and all the responses it has ever given are in mere samples of life's very minute and early works. Students find a very small "cell" which is the first visible work of every life starting to form itself a body within that of its own parent, either animal or vegetable. The cell itself is not life, but the body of a life commenced upon the same plan as its parents' life was commenced before it. The "cell" does not differ much in all the various kinds of life known, either animal or vegetable, great or small. The earnest student with his microscope sees the live cell, a very minute structure, but the beginning of a life has already passed and the microscope is confronted with just a sample of life's work, just a little cell with fluid centre rapidly forming and connecting other matter by cells and combinations, and growing apace until the time comes for a separate existence from its parent, or for some marked transformation. For example, among winged insects that deposit their eggs where there is food for a worm, the life in the egg first deposited in the food begins and organizes a worm body that eats of that food and grows to maturity and then passes into the chrysalis state where the matter in its worm body is, some of it rejected and some of it used as food for the same life to organize and to mature a body of the insect kind which being completed with wings, the insect, it may be a butterfly, comes out in the real likeness of its own true parents, and ready in due time and in similar manner to deposit eggs for the starting of other animals, but of its own kind only. All created lives have their own kind of transformations from embryo or germ to final maturity, but the metamorphoses of insects are so unique and visible as to be best known. We think of the butterfly going away with a bright new body and wings to fly in the air from its decayed chrysalis, and we wonder if it knows or remembers anything about its former mode of life as a disgusting worm. Does it know how it once crawled as a worm and then slept as a chrysalis before it awoke in the air on wings with all its attractive adornments of form and color and blithe motions? These are simple hints of the transformations, sleeps, torpors, and encasements which show that life is capable of a continued existence in some organisms and in some circumstances that indicate a very limited degree of activity. It is said that life is action; but when we take two kernels of wheat from an old-time harvest and plant them, if one grows and the other does not, we say only one of those seeds was a live seed. Still life, in its own nature as a substantive existence, is something distinct from—I do not say separable from—all its changes and all its works, however wonderful they may be. We see it only while in some of its works and these show it to be a self-directing agent, bringing things seen out of the unseen, manifesting itself in either animal or vegetable forms and always after the type of its own kind; never visible until it makes itself **so by its own** growth **in its** own natural organisms. All seeds have the stamp of their progenitors, so that **every kind of life started in the world has a continuous** likeness to its original by natural parentage, however much it may be increased in numbers; and though it does become modified in time by its historical conditions, climate, food, **works and surroundings** yet the tendency of all lives under like conditions **is towards the** likeness **of the** original from **which they came; organisms like** organisms, and character like character. Natural parentage is more potent **than** " natural selection."

Again there are many time periods **of life** which distinguish it from the laws of matter. **Some lives manifest their presence** in matter **for one day—ephemera—and some for 3,000 years,** (the cedars of Lebanon,) and **this is a** characteristic **circumstance of life. Even** disease **germs, microbes, are estimated to** have their respective periods of incubation, upon the same principle of larger organisms.

Notice also that the laws of matter, cohesion, gravitation, electricity, heat, magnetism, chemical affinity, etc., all continue their force in organized matter the same as in unorganized; and yet withal we see that there is no life in the world so humble and lowly. There is nothing known as a life that does not do works with the laws of matter, that these laws or forces cannot do without the life force. For example, an apple tree will cause to appear upon twigs from its branches 500 pounds of apples in five months, from May to October. With the law of gravitation for the whole time in persistent opposition to there being a single ounce of apples up there. We see the apples as solids, every atom in them is now obedient to the law of cohesion, and in some way has been taken by life from the law of repulsion and diffusion and prepared by growth to be presented visibly in fruit as we now see them. These are works of life so common that we scarcely stop to think of them; but they are enough to show that life works, as works, are easily distinguishable from any and all the laws and works of physical forces. If anyone says the laws of capillary attraction fed the tree and the fruit, we have only to look at a tree without life and see if it feeds apples or anything else.

We are all familiar with the process of grafting trees, and we know that whether the whole tree is grafted or only a part, the graft grows in wood fiber, looks and fruit of its own native kind.

The graft produces its own proper kind of fruit, while the roots and body of the tree in which it is placed render all needed service in the fluid circulations required by the graft. The graft retains its own nature and does its own characteristic work in fruit bearing of its own kind. By this we see that the shoots, twigs and leaves of trees control their roots and bodies as to what their work shall be in fruit bearing, and the body and roots of the tree become simply contributory. This is a pleasing result, when we see a worthless tree made valuable by grafting into it a little scion from a good tree; and in like manner a worthless scion may be grafted into a good tree; and grafting may accomplish conversion and re-conversion, but no third kind or new kind of fruit can be obtained by grafting, but rather one of the strongest evidences of the tendency of all life to be faithful to its ancestral type. Life is always dependent upon the co-operation of all the laws of matter, notwithstanding its own higher character and power. Whenever any matter suited to any particular life ceases agreeably to its own laws to serve reasonably well, life after a brief struggle gives up the contest, leaves its own organism and passes to some other state, condition or place. To our limited knowledge it disappears. Likewise its organism, its body, passes in due time to some other condition of matter. We can follow the decomposition of the organism, every atom of it, back to its former state of fluid and solid elements of matter. Obedient still to all.

those laws, but free now from the law of life. Probably if we could follow it we should find in like manner the reversion of vegetable life to its former normal condition in space, or that the life of the dying reverts again to a condition in space similar to what it had with its kind before it became constituted in matter by its own organization therein. Whenever matter is in a perfectly prepared condition to receive life there is always a kind of universal presence of it to start organisms, and we can see no reason why it should not come forth again and again in such kind of organisms as by the laws of its creation God has predetermined it. There is no spontaneous generation, but in the due order of nature there is always some kind of life present to all matter in a fit condition to receive it. A plant in dying retires from its own body and leaves it to the laboratory of nature to be chemically and mechanically prepared for reorganization, and this is constantly going on under our own observation. The bones and shells of many animals may continue in some places undissolved; but not in places where the air, heat, water and life are constantly acting upon them. This known reversion of the elements of matter, and the identical atoms of it, back and forth between the seen and unseen, or the solids and fluids, shows that life does not increase or diminish the quantity of matter existing. If life should organize all the matter of the world it would not add one atom to what is now existing. It would simply change its form and modify or re-refine its character. Neither does it seem likely that the lower grades of life, as plant life, for example, has not the same facility of reversion back and forth between matter in which it becomes organized and a place and state of existence in which it is not organized, as its own organism has of reversion of all its elements to their former state after life's departure from them. The question is whether life is not furnished to plant organisms in some way analogous to that in which matter is furnished from its unseen atoms. As life is even more retired into the unseen, when out of its organisms, than fluid matter is when out of the same, why should not the former have a relative place of existence in the unseen fluids of the invisible part of the world as well as the latter in the seen things of the world and without any necessity of being a material substance? Why should not life be increased to the plant as it needs it, as well as invisible atoms as it needs them? The plant increases by atoms of matter taken from the air every day. Why not the increase of its life in a similar manner? I can see no reason for thinking that any of the lower kinds of life, either vegetable or animal, ever actually leave this world, if we understand the world to include the air space belonging to it. Life is never manifested but where fluids are in circulation in a visible organism, but its presence wherever matter is ready for organization and a seed is rightly inserted seems to be as universal as the air itself.

I am the more explicit in this matter because I do not regard the highest order of life as included in this or in any like reversions or system of renewals. Man's circuit includes his accountability to God in this life and that which is to come. Heb. 9: xxvii: "It is appointed unto man once to die, but after that the judgment." Man, in the image of God, has a continued identity of person and character; for him we find not only that "the body returns to dust as it was and the spirit to God who gave it," but that God will bring every work into judgment, whether it be good or evil."—Eccl. 12: vii and xiv. Science knows of no possible way in which annihilation can take place in any atom of matter whatever. Changes of relative quantities and varieties of combinations, forms and changes of place, are all that matter or atoms of matter are capable of showing. And so of life in its lower orders. It may have changes of place and varied conditions of existence, with endless variety in forms; and this, with its works, is all we know of it. Its conception, and growth, and form, and work, and death we see, while all the rest of its circuit is hid from us, though not without a clear hint of its reversion into the fluid space from which it came.

The question as to when life first appeared in our world is one of considerable interest, from a geological point of view, because the structure of the earth's crust shows so much work done by life organisms in producing the solids as we now find them, that to fix the date of rocks and conglomerate formations is to fix a date of life for the organisms in those formations. Fossil remains are found entombed in the rocks; petrified remains are found in places eight miles below the earth's surface. These give us the certainty of teeming millions of plants and animals in each successive step of the world's career. From the view we have taken of the transformation of a part of the world's materials from a fluid into a solid state by compression and cohesion, which made the earth for awhile a ball of fire with an outwardly overspread darkness of smoke, it is plain that life could not have been manifested in the first period of the world's cooling down process. Time enough must have elapsed for a portion of its vapor and smoke to have become liquefied before a habitable place was ready for any kind of life, as we now see it. Even the aquatic plants and shell-forming animals required delay for the earth to cool down; but the moment that took place we can imagine the word to have gone forth and that self-multiplying organisms, life organisms, prevailed to the extent of the world's preparedness for their work. At the first there could have been no pure water and no pure air, agreeably to our present ideas. Purification required separations and rejections. Not until the chemical processes of nature had ceased to be violent universally, and the extreme solids that could stand the highest degrees of heat and the liquid solutions that would first condense were parting from each other, would there be any place or any sustenance for life; no conditions of matter in a state of readiness to receive it in the places where it now exists. Doubtless our Heavenly Father saw the world ready for life before He spoke the word that brought it here, and in just the kinds for its first introduction. Some kinds could endure a high degree of heat, some could exist in liquids but poorly aerified, all had a peculiar work to do in getting the world ready for the higher order of beings—workers whose bodies were to become so large a part of the crust and soils needed for future occupants. There was no reason why these should wait after the conditions of the temperature and sustenance admitted of their presence. The wonderful life organisms in the shape of mammoth plants and trees, gigantic animals, megatheriums and other monsters, as well as smaller crustaceans and polyps, an immense throng of countless varieties, all along the past ages are now presented in the crusts of the earth and described in our text books of geology. We have fossil remains, both flora and fauna, in every strata of the earth's crust since the first, or certainly the second, showing that life had been in the world from the earliest time, and of such kinds as it could support in all its own changing conditions. The carbon and lime that existed in a gaseous state as fluids at first needed to be removed from the air, and life was made the appointed agency for removing it. Plants and animals made their own bodies mostly of these materials; there was carbon enough for all the plants and lime enough for all the shells and bones and coral reefs. The lives that solidified all these immense quantities of carbon and lime have left their record in the rocks and chalk formations, in the coal mines and coral reefs, witnessing of what the humblest lives once did to prepare the world for the needs of men. Aquatic plants and mollusca and polyps may have filled many waters when but little soil or rock was dry—perhaps before the firmament was a visible reality and the waters began to be purified in the way we now see it, in its circuits to the sky and through gravel beds of earth to fresh springs and fountains, a present delight to the children of men, a necessity to the present animal kingdom.

We have seen before that all lives make their own bodies and begin the same invisibly in the living bodies from which they descend. We now observe, that all characteristics of every kind become known of what kind they are only as the life and growth of animals and plants reveal them. In the very lowest grades of vegetables and animals both are respectively so near alike that science has not determined the class of all of them whether animal or vegetable. A school of polyps building a coral island in a southern sea may strongly resemble a flower garden on the land. The protozoa, among which we find the sponge, are very closely allied to some vegetable forms, yet from thence in the upward scale, vegetable and animal begin to diverge and keep on diverging until their contrasts become as immeasurable as their first characters were indistinguishable. There is no comparison between a blooming buttercup in the meadow and an elephant that tramps his foot upon it; yet if we trace them back to the germs and microscopic embryo of their existence simply as germs we find them not much apart in their vitalized atoms of matter. To us they start from an invisible line of separation as they take their respective departures out of the unseen fluid. The one, by the way predetermined by its vegetable parentage, to become a butter cup in the meadow and the other by the way of an animal parentage to become an elephant.

One of the first things in which vegetables and animals are seen to differ is in food taking for their own growth. Plants take in their food at innumerable pores in their roots and leaves and they do not show us any visible way in which they reject or eject any refuse matter. Very low animals, by a kind of muscular vibration, draw in their food with more or less extraneous matter at one or more mouths about their bodies in various places, from which also they expel what is rejected and either internally or externally construct solids—bones, coral or shells. There is not much in a miscroscopic foraminifera to show the whole scale of the animal kingdom, neither is there much in a microscopic plant to show the magnitude of the vegetable kingdom. So little does organized matter in its first degree differ from the unorganized of similar kind that it is difficult in some instances to tell whether certain matter is moved by life or only by electricity, magnetism, heat or some other merely physical force. We have seen before that all seen things are made from unseen, and that all lives make their own bodies and forms and faculties in the use of invisible atoms of matter. We now notice that the upward grade of faculties and forms from one kind of life to another, in both kingdoms, is by steps that are invisibly small when singly examined, showing us again and again that the seen is from the unseen. If we take a systematic botany and start on the ascending scale a tour through the vegetable kingdom we shall take 100,000 steps, more or less, before we arrive at the highest specimen of vegetable life. Or if we choose to take a text book on Zoology and make the tour of the animal kingdom we shall have a larger number of steps, probably a million, if we begin with microcosms, before we reach the highest order of animals. But one thing we shall see long before we arrive at the superlative of either of these two kinds of life, that the vegetable is for the use of the animal kingdom.

The lilies and all the vegetable adornments of the world, the cedar and all the precious timber-making trees, the vine and all the fruit-bearing trees of the world, the golden harvests of grain and all food products of the vegetable are for the use of a higher, that is, the animal kingdom—a feast of fat things and a necessity to their existence. Yet the vegetable kingdom loses nothing when it is used by animals for which it was made. A fair equivalent is made by animals in the cultivation of the soil—worms, ants, rodents numberless, and the whole animal kingdom give back what the vegetable needs more than it does its own fruit. There are also resemblances and contrasts of character all along the rising scale of both kingdoms. Good and evil are always near each other and in contradiction in all the places in the world wherever we take our observations.

Another fact of life is its labor necessity and its wants. There is no physical life known to us that was ever intended to live without labor and food. Life comes into the world with abounding wants, and the higher the life the higher the wants. The tiniest foraminifer, with its microscopic shell, has its wants; wants supplied, by which it has already made its own little house thus far, and wants continuing, by which it will enlarge its house a little and then multiply its own kind before it dies. Its wants were only a little liquid, but that was so real that without it it could not have multiplied its own kind or left, in dying, a beautiful microscopic shell as a sample of its skill to surprise and instruct the wisest of men for ages to come in the chalk beds of England. But as we turn with upward glances toward a higher and larger kind of aquatic animals wants are multiplied apace. It is not a mere drop of lime or saline water that a whale requires; but, with his enormous mouth open, he must swim through whole schools of small aquatic animals and engulf them by myriads into his capacious chest and there digest them and transform them into flesh and oil and whalebone for the use of men.

And so there is an index finger in every life pointing to a transformation work to be done in the attainment of a useful end in the service of men. The earth itself were a useless thing by itself alone, with no end to serve, for all values are determined where transfers are made, and until life came into the world there was nothing to make matter valuable; but life has use for it and need of it. So the only fair deduction is that God made the material world for the use of the living world, and hence that He purposed at the first what to have in his finished work at the last, and included all the requisite means for its accomplishment. The Divine object and plan of creation opens Godward plainer and brighter with each new day. The principle of contrasts is universal in matter and in life organized in matter. Solids are seen in contrast with fluids, organized matter in contrast with unorganized, friendly plants and friendly lives in contrast with unfriendly plants and animals, good trees in contrast with briars, weeds and thistles; domestic animals in contrast with vipers and scorpions —animals not made for willing service of men, but to excite their watchfulness and defence against them. All over the world, up and down the walks of men, these contrasts are at hand striving for the mastery. Unfriendly lives are all furnished, directly or indirectly, with offensive and defensive arms and supplies of energy for the conflict. It is not a true view of the plan of creation to imagine that conflicts among sentient beings were never intended. The true view is that conflicts are the subject matter of a perfect law of righteousness, and when these occur where they ought not they are a sin against God and the forfeit of His blessing. But to imagine that a man is not to destroy the weeds in his garden, or the wild wolf at his hen roost, is a false view of the use we should make of means God has provided for our education, development and character, manliness and courage. Yea, even our Godliness requires this. We take no adequate measure of the usefulness of enemies until we see that no human character was ever perfected without them; the duties of life are modified by them, and moral government obtains its meaning from their existence; they excite us to watchfulness, and make us feel our need of Divine care and guidance. If our enemies are men, and our obedience to God can make them friends, we have great joy in their recovery. If they are creatures of a lower order of beings, injurious to men, they should be expelled from human abodes, if need be, by the forfeit of their lives. The ravenous wolf has no place in the nursery with the Shepherd's tender children, neither with His precious lambs in the flock.

Whoever is a friend to all the good beings there are in the world must needs be an enemy to all the evil and prepared with the "whole armor of God to resist it."—Eph. vi : 13. I deem it a false sentiment to think of the broad universal contrasts and conflicts in this world as an oversight or an accident under God, who is calling us up to Himself and away from these conflicts when our characters are perfected by giving our love and allegiance to our Heavenly Father above all else. "This is our victory that overcometh the world, even our faith in God."—I John, v : 4.

Besides vegetable and animal life there are

two other and higher kinds that have come into the world since the first two came, and they grade upward from animal life after the same manner that all life grades upward from unorganized matter. There are certain possibilities in mineral matter when acted upon by electricity that give an appearance of forms and motions made by life. They are forms scarcely distinguishable from organized matter, although entirely destitute of any functional capacity whatever. From this low mineral base life begins and grades upward, while it spreads abroad in endless varieties, until the highest order of vegetable and animal life is reached; then human life, coming next in order, grades upward as well. It differs in the lowest from the mere animal life in its combinations of intellectual and moral faculties; its self-government is expressed in laws that mere animal life cannot comprehend—there is a moral meaning in the words "right and wrong" which no mere animal can ever know. A horse may be taught to observe the landmarks of his owner's field, but not for the reason that the Eighth Commandment would be violated by pasturing upon another man's lot. Man is capable of a greater variety of studies, and of obtaining different and higher knowledge, than can be predicated of animals; he is a more intelligent and comprehensive character; he is capable of forming ideals of beauty and of improvement in character; he is capable of feeling a difference between right and wrong, and of willing to do the right; he is capable of rendering obedience to the laws that grade upward from the material and common things of this world to the highest spiritual and eternal verities of the Divine Father's revealed will. Man's life grades downward through all the laws of matter; his very blood has atoms of iron in it; his lungs require great volumes of air every day, perhaps 20,000 gallons of air every day for mere breathing purposes; a great user of matter is the physical man for his food and drink. And now, turning upward, the next order of life above the human is the spiritual life. This differs from the human in its conscious relations to God in a higher degree than is common to human life; the spiritual relations to God as a spirit are more distinctly realized and personally felt; the spiritual life has knowledge in its own experience which did not come to it by the words of men or the persuasions of men alone, but by the realized presence of the Divine being and the assurance of a personal responsibility to Him. Hence the spiritual is closer to God than the human life, or any former state of man's experience in his relations to God, so that sin appears more sinful and righteousness more blessed. The spiritual life desires the will of God to be done on earth as it is in heaven, and it rejoices in righteousness wherever it is found among men; it includes greater faith in God and a more comprehensive righteousness in regard to both God and men. With such, and many more evidences of being born of God, man's life may rise upward to its crowning height of a spiritual being, with spiritual faculties and sensibilities—a child of God and heir to eternal life. "Called, not to be conformed to this world, but to be transformed by the renewing of our minds, that we may prove what is that good and acceptable and perfect will of God,"—Romans xii: 2. The experience of this life in doing the will of God "is righteousness and peace and joy in the Holy Ghost." The work to be done is the upbuilding of character in the spiritual kingdom by the conversion of men to Christ. Our estimate of spiritual things is above all earthly values, so that, by contrast, the world is not regretted either as it passes away or remains with its disciplinary experiences in the school of Christ. There is, therefore, consistency in the plan that holds the body to earth for a time but allows the mind, by faith and hope and love, to converse in heaven and to strive for a greater fitness to meet the glorified Lord and to see Him as He is—"the Son of God and the son of man,.

who came that we might have life, and that we might have it more abundantly."—John x : 10.

We should not forget that all moral character is formed on the human side and grows by free-will acts, by acts of choice at the time they were done. When moral evil is found it is seen as the result of a voluntary opposition to or a departure from the revealed will of God. In the lower kingdoms we find friends and enemies to men, in the world of humanity we find friends and enemies to God. The unavoidable result of our personal freedom of moral action is that we must gravitate to one or the other of these two classes—friends or enemies to God. It is not an arbitrary arrangement, but universally arrived at by free will from first to last—hence the necessity of growth and progress in a spiritual life, so as to pass beyond the condition of conflict and to obtain unto righteousness, joy and peace in the Father's house in heaven. The "way, the truth and the life" is preached alike to all men and always on condition of a ruling faith in our Lord and Redeemer, who will save to the uttermost all who come unto God by Him "who died for us and rose again."—II Cor., v: 15.

"**For** the commandment is a lamp, and the law is light." —Prov. 6:23.

LAWS AND COUNTER LAWS.

CHAPTER IV.

In all scientific studies known phenomena must be referred to known laws, and newly discovered phenomena must be reported in some way as a farther revelation of laws, for in science there is nothing without law. Hence we speak of the law of gravitation, the law of the repulsion of atoms and the diffusion of the same; the law of the cohesion of atoms, the law of chemical affinity, the law of definite proportions in chemical compounds; the law of momentum, the law of the reflection of light and of the radiation of the same; the law of combustion and of heat, electricity, galvanism, magnetism, polarization, crystallization; the laws of colors and of the blending of colors; and of numerous other laws known to science in the conduct of matter and classified to facilitate farther studies of the same or like subjects. To know the laws of nature is to have the keys to all its treasures, the treasures of the world. The creation was by laws, and the whole world is held to them; so that we can only know the world by its laws, and ourselves by the laws of our own existence. The doors to knowledge are hung on laws and opened and closed by them; so, as fast as we know the laws of nature, they are for our use, security, enjoyment and well being; an inheritance for all the human race and for all time to come. So far as we have any means of knowing all laws are eternal, and more and more beneficent in proportion as they are respected and obeyed and their Author loved and glorified.

We need clear views of what we understand by the word law, when we apply it to the conduct of unconscious matter. When we use the word in relation to men with intelligence, freedom of will and power to act as they will, we mean by *Law* some definite rule or rules of conduct to be performed by subjects owing obedience to the government or ruler by whom they are governed, and by whom the law was decreed and enjoined. The word implies a government with a constitution or system of rules for its subjects to obey. Five things are manifest. The government, the laws, the subjects, the obedience due and the manner of enforcing it with the rewards and penalties.

So in like manner in the conduct of matter. Any rule to which it is always found to conform in all its changes of state and condition, just as if obligated to do so by some efficient cause governing it, is properly called a law. And there is no better word in science and none better understood, except as to the reason why matter does act so in conformity to rules. Why does every atom of matter and cluster of atoms, known to men, go and come always in all its changes in conformity to rules with a promptness and certainty that commands our admiration and confidence in spite of all its wonderful mysteriousness to our comprehension? We see unconscious matter obeying laws and revealing the same to us for our use and guidance. What a phenomenon is this! Where can we find the adequate cause for this conduct of unconscious matter? We may listen for an answer from the earth, and many are seeking and waiting for an answer to come from matter itself just where it is manifested. But we must not confound the phenomenon and its cause, or make them both one and indistinguishable. Of course we see the conduct of matter in itself; there is nowhere else to see it. But to say that unconscious matter acts in itself because it acts so of itself is not scientific, and not as ingenuous as to confess ignorance. Better by far to refer it at once to the Infinite One above us, the Creator of all things, "in whom we live and move and have our being."

Let us, therefore, answer reverently that all we know of the cause of conformity to laws as we see it in unconscious matter is that God has obviously made it so, and predetermined all such matter to obey laws by a necessity of its own nature. This facility of matter to obey laws, this responsiveness to definite rules and the same atom of matter so endowed as to obey a very great variety of laws, is of God; and is like all direct acts of His, grand in its manifestations and comprehensiveness. We recognize its unspeakable value, cannot imagine how the world could abide for a moment without it, and still we feel that the way of it is incomprehensible to our finite minds.

Any act of God is all powerful within the limits He gave it to the end of time. So of this endowment of unconscious matter with ability to conform to law; its Author had a way by which He made it so to do. We do not know how He did it. We account for many things by referring them to the wills and ability of the actors; but here in unsconscious matter there is no will, and yet we see it fulfilling the requirements of law more strictly than subjects that have will.

If we trace the evidences of free will from man downward all along down the lower grades of life to its vanishing point in unconscious matter, where no law can receive an obedience from any free will, instinct or tendency of freedom, we find in matter itself an absolute necessity of obedience to law pure and simple ; and that necessity of obedience not to one law alone, but to all the laws of matter as in turn it becomes qualified to serve one after another in all the processes and changes of nature. Is not this of God? And possibly no harder for Him than to make man with free will, and after that, by placing him under a necessity for some self-government in the use of that gift and to show him that he has it, to hold him as a subject of both necessity and free will, combined and harmonized in the highest perfection of faith. That is, the whole man and all his race as a true subject of all his laws and yet as his children of free will. The one need not surprise us more than the other. Both are unspeakably surprising and undeniably true.

All the laws of nature are acts of God, and because they are His acts they continue forever without any possibility of pause or change, except in the will of the Creator. He alone can repeal what He, Himself, has decreed. When a rule is given by an act or word of His, all atoms of matter within the limits of that rule must be subject to His government and obey forever and everywhere that rule, simply because the efficiency of an act of God has no limitations but in His own will. God said, "Let there be light," and that act of God was a law to all atoms of matter of every kind concerned in light being, to be subject to that rule for all time to come.

All acts of God are eternal if He wills them so. Man throws a stone and, whether he wills it or not, it falls to the ground within a limited time. God throws the whole world and it goes on its orbit to the end of time, because gravitation is an act of God. He turns the world on its axis and it has never ceased to turn, for the obvious reason that He has not stopped it and there is no one else that can stop it.

A law of nature is a strict rule of action, to which the same kind of matter, under the same circumstances, will always conform. It is more than a tendency in matter so to act. We can and do trust our lives upon it and feel there is a certainty that it will do again and again just what it did before, with all the conditions precisely the same, and we dare not trust them for anything else, however much we may desire a deviation on special occasions. We see the laws through the extreme accuracy with which they are kept, and we ascribe them to God the same as we do the creation of the world itself; all these are His acts and the world creation includes them. Howbeit, the omnipresent God must be imminent in all His laws and yet distinct from them. "In Him we live and move and have our being," yet we are distinct from Him. "God is a Spirit."

Our view of law relations to matter is that all things are at all times under all the laws of matter, and that any given atom, or mass of atoms, may at one time be more prominently and manifestly under one law, and at another time prominently under another law; but that all things are law subjects and constantly within the scope of all the laws of matter and of nature, from which no atom ever has had, or ever can have, any freedom of nature to escape. All the laws of nature are constant and unchangeable, but all the matter in the world is inconstant and changeable, subject to new conditions, combinations and transformations and re-combinations. What may be the higher or manifest law to any given matter in one point of time may not be so in the next, for there is always a higher law present, whenever there is any matter ready to receive it. Matter may change rapidly from one law to another, as it becomes fitted for such changes of manifestation, for it is a law of all the laws to take matter that is fitted to respond obediently in service to its rule and no other. The changes by which matter passes from one law to another must always take place in itself and not in the laws. All the mechanisms of nature, with all the forces of the same, are working on in their respective spheres in the preparation of matter, in the getting it ready to pass from one higher law to another in its rounds of services in nature. Fire, water, life, sunlight and darkness, air and chemical forces of endless variety and power, with electricty, are working in and with matter to get it in condition and ready to obey other higher laws, just as fast as its finished work, under present laws, will permit it so to do.

In all these processes with matter we see the law of rejection, as well as the law of acceptance, manifested all the way down to the lowest conditions of matter; only a part of any divided mass ever goes at once to the same law. Purification of matter implies dividing and separating the pure from the impure, yet neither part, in such a case, escapes in the least from law, for there is no atom of any kind of matter that does not reveal in itself the evidence of conformity to one or more laws. When we see a snowflake we recognize at once five or more laws of matter revealed in it: 1st.—Cohesion, or we could not see it. 2nd.—Congelation, or it would be a liquid drop and not a snowflake. 3rd.—Crystallization, or its charming mathematical forms of angles would not appear. 4th.—The reflection of light, or its radiant beauty would be wanting. 5th.—Gravitation, or it would not descend. Gravitation brings it down. Heat melts it and turns it into water. More heat evaporates it into mist; then still finer mist, even fluid, and now it obeys the law of repulsion and diffusion and so passes away in the opposite direction from what gravitation would take it, and of course by a law that is opposite to gravitation. Gravitation is seen in matter moving or tending to move toward the centre of the earth, and our snow-flake, aided by heat, is now free from that law, and having gone farther from mist to real fluid, and passing as fluid into the service of the law of repulsion, is now in millions of atoms, a numerous fleet, sailing upward through the air towards the firmament above, and the fact that we do not see it going up is our witness that it is free from cohesion in very deed, free from congelation, free from crystallization, free from reflecting light and free from gravitation—though it may soon come again under these or some of these laws, unless it is caught in a fog, or joins its forces in some descending rain drops, or is drawn off into some work of vegetation, or is quaffed by some animal in breathing, or is yet driven of the winds on some long excursion. No laws are more opposite than repulsion and cohesion, yet enormous quantities of matter are passing and re-passing every moment from one state to the other, not by their own conflicts alone; heat and cold and life are very prominent agencies. All the forces of nature have their due part in all such changes. If the atoms in any solid form are to be made ready to serve repulsion they must be reduced by heat, or, in some way, be pulverized to an impalpable dust till its atoms are freed from cohesion. I repeat, matter is never taken by a law it is not fitted to manifest and serve. Its fitness of condition, its preparedness to obey, is the ground of its election to any new service or higher law.

All matter goes at once from one law to another as fast as it is made ready so to do. What is trampled under foot of men to-day may in due time appear in the tints of a rose or in the happy, bright eyes of a young philosopher; for there is in the world vast opportunities for fluid matter to keep up a circuit of changes; that is to say, to new services under laws. There is no dignity in matter itself, except in the laws it reveals and honors. Environments changes matter but not laws. We may take a diamond from a king's crown and place it in oxygen gas and touch it with a match and it will flame up at once and all will become carbonic acid gas, yet no law in the world has changed a particle. I take in my hand a lump of anthracite. Here are atoms of carbon manifestly subject to the law of cohesion in this lump of coal, and they obey the law of gravitation by falling from my hand down upon the fire on the grate, where, submitting to the law of combustion, they are expelled by heat force up the chimney into the air and serve obediently under the law of repulsion of heat and cold and air currents until they arrive at a living tree, when the law of vegetable life gives to them a fit place in the leaves of the tree, to serve the laws of life and of cohesion and of color and of gravitation and of the winds that blow upon it, first one way and then another, until a camel comes along and browses the leaf and it then submits to the law of mastication and digestion, the law of liquids and of veinous and arterial circulation, the law of assimilation and other laws of animal life, until the law of ejectments gets it in the breath or perspiration or some other of the animal's refuses, when it may pass under some chemical law of combination and solution to the root or leaves of a rose bush and serve the law of life then a while and finally appear in some beautiful tints of the full-blown rose, perhaps to be gathered and passed to the compounder of attar of roses, and then to become choice perfumery for some lady's toilet. All I wish or aim to say now is that material atoms are always subject to any law they are prepared for, and they never do serve, or continue to serve, any law they are not prepared for and put in condition to serve and obey. The atoms of carbon in a lump of coal cannot be subject to any law of life until they are set free from the law of cohesion. No law of life ever appropriates atoms finally until they are reduced to a fluid state. I do not say that animal organisms are not provided with means of reducing solids to fluids, but we have before seen that all things that are made, or grow, are made in the use of atoms, pre-existing in a fluid state ; that the fluid state is maintained by the law of repulsion, and the solid state by the law of cohesion. Separate from these two laws, exactly opposite to each other, there is no life organism, and hence no law of life manifested to us where either of these laws are absent. There are swarms of life organisms so small as to be scarcely visible in their individuality, and not one of these could live in one state of matter alone. Fluid alone cannot constitute an organism, and a solid alone cannot nourish one and keep it alive.

There runs through nature a co-operation of laws notwithstanding their opposites, and there is nothing known to us that does not manifest obedience to two or more laws of nature, however rapidly it may pass from one to another. The law of cohesion of matter is the most manifest in things visible as they now are; and the holding of atoms together makes it possible for them to obey the law of gravitation. The withdrawal of cohesion would leave the whole visible world, including our own bodies, to fall back again into invisible atoms, "without form and void." All the variety and beauty there is in the world would vanish in a moment. There could be no such thing as form, or color, without cohesion. Light, itself, can have no color until it touches some surface where cohesion exists. All this is but one thing in the value of one of the laws by which the Creator governs the material universe. We can think of laws separately, but it is vain to imagine that they have ever existed separately since the beginning of the creation.

We notice that laws of nature are uniform wherever we may go. That is, anything that is subject to any given law is subject to the same law under the same conditions everywhere. A body that is subject to the law of gravitation on the land is subject to the same law on the sea, and in the air, and to the farthest of globes yet seen by the telescope. There is not a new law or a different law of gravitation in one place from another, but the law is one and always the same, under the same conditions of matter to obey it. And so of the law of repulsion and of cohesion. As far as any telescope can enable us to observe, there is the same law of repulsion that ministers to our world, serving all worlds throughout the universe, and the same law of cohesion that makes the solids of our earth what they are—makes all existing solids wherever they are. It is not one law here that makes atoms free in space and another law at the stars, and it is not one law here that holds atoms together, and makes solids capable of gravitation, and another law at the moon that makes that capable of gravitation. And so of the laws of light, and of darkness, and of heat, and of cold. They have no local limitations as laws. They are not local to the world as laws, have no power in one place that they have not in all places, under the same circumstances, with the same matter with which they have to do. Upon the retina of our eyes the light falls as readily from the distant Sirius as from the near Venus. To know the laws of light in one world is probably to know them in all worlds under like conditions. That the government of all the material worlds, under the same Creator, are by the same laws we have no reason to doubt.

Whatever is to be the subject of any given law, at any given place, must be made ready for it, be exactly conditioned and prepared for it. Every law of nature knows its own subjects on the instant. If the law of gravitation finds a boy on the limb of a tree too weak to hold him, it claims the right to take that boy a quick and direct passage towards the centre of the earth to the next station, and we have never felt any surprise that it does the same thing with an apple in the same circumstances, when its stem is insufficient to hold it. We see precisely the same rule in all the other laws of nature; none takes but that which is in condition to obey it. If sunlight finds a sensative plate all ready for a photograph, the camera and plate all ready in their due places, and a boy presents his face in due manner, an outline of the boy's face will be made on the glass. Thus are the laws of nature for the use of men on condition of co-operation in preparing for them. Give the sunlight an opportunity and it will show its willingness to serve men. Prof. Henry remarked in his day—"A man might spend a lifetime in the study of one ray of light and do good service for men."

If we look at laws in their contrasts, and classify them by contrasts, we can always put with any given law of nature another law that is exactly contrary to the first in all their manifestations in the material world. For example, take **repulsion** and **cohesion**. Cohesion holds atoms of matter together and keeps them solid, (its distinctive work is always in that direction and no other,) while repulsion drives atoms apart aud keeps them fluid, (that is its distinctive work always and everywhere.)

And so of all other laws of matter. There are those, when considered alone, that tend to final results of extremest unlikeness. At the exact point of starting, the two are together, and the difference in work is least, if perceptible ; then moving from the neutral, their opposites become immeasurable. Let cohesion begin to manifest itself in cooling steam, turning it into mist, a very thin fog, then a denser fog, and then into water, then ice and the hardest possible ice ; while in the opposite direction from the place of starting, the beginning of repulsion is seen in changing the fog to a lighter density and then to invisibility in the clear atmosphere, higher and higher up, becoming more and more attenuated as the law works farther and farther away towards its own supremacy of power in the repulsion of atoms, far from one another in the thin ether beyond the skies. Such opposite works are common to all the laws of nature when considered in this way by their distinctive contrasts. No solid can be more solid than the law of cohesion prescribes, and no fluid can be more fluid than the law of repulsion prescribes. The solid rock may be an example on the one side of cohesion, and the lightest ether above the skies for the extreme repulsion of atoms; while between these opposite extremes of work, done conformably to the two opposite laws, all other matter in the world must be classified in respect to its hardness or fluidity by degrees of subjection to either one or the other of these two laws. A solid may be so near fluid that we cannot place it, and a fluid may be so near solid that its true state is uncertain.

Let us bear in mind that this difference is not because one has mineral atoms and the other has not, for both have that. And it is not because one law is stronger than the other, for both are infinite in the matter prepared for them. And it is not because they do not start out from one and the same place, or from one common, invisible and neutral point, but it is because their outgoing is in opposite directions. If we grade solids up towards the fluids, and fluids down towards the solids, we shall come to matter so neutral that science does not know which law it is obeying, and still we feel that no atom of matter can conform manifestly to these two opposite laws at one and the same time. Every atom of matter in the universe belongs, at each moment of time, to either a fluid or a solid state, and not to both at the same time.

In some instances outgoing forces in matter are simultaneous in opposite directions. They are ascribed to one law, and the opposites in its action are said to be, the one positive and the other negative; as when we say of the magnet—the end that attracts is positive, and the end that repels is negative. "Like poles repel and unlike poles attract." So of electricity—there are two kinds always present; the one kind is said to be positive and the other negative, and all substances manifesting electricity are said to be electro-positive or electro-negative, in relation to each other, according to the electricity they contain at the time of the experiment. Here, again, **is the same law;** unlike electricity attracts and like electricity repels. **However** this simultaneousness of opposite actions in **the same manner is not commonly manifested precisely in that way, neither do we** know positively **that there are not as** many **laws in electricity** and magnetism as **these** contrary actions. The visible material in **which they** act is not altered. Commonly opposite **laws in matter are known** by actions and changes that do alter its form and condition, and therefore cannot both be **manifested as working supremely in** a small **particle of it at the same time and place, as magnetism and electricity do.** We can find no magnet **so** small **as not** to have its two poles and two kinds **of action. The mag**net's two states **are always in** its own little **self, as well as in the two poles of the** world.

Heat and cold are not simultaneous and

co-present in the same sense and manner. They do not touch each other everywhere in the same degree all the time in the same atoms of matter. They are not both in the one place at the same time in equal force. Heat and cold, as opposites to each other, are present in the same matter only in the relative degrees of force. The two are in a state of resistance everywhere, pushing each other as contending forces through all the seasons of the year, and in all the elements of nature. When we wish to help the cold in the pitcher of water on the table we douse a piece of ice into the water, and that reinforces the cold. Again, if we desire more warmth of air in our study, we increase the furnace fire and that reinforces the heat.

Atoms in some way act in obedience to the law of heat, or the law of cold, so that only one shall occupy the same atom of matter supremely at the same time and place, though both forces are present in relative degrees. In this, as in all other contrasts, there is somewhere an initial point, a neutrality from which both heat and cold started, and from which heat goes off in one direction and cold in the other, in exact conformity to all known laws in matter to their extremest unlikeness. Heat reaches somewhere in one direction its highest degree of temperature in matter, and cold in the opposite direction reaches somewhere its lowest degree of temperature in matter. And all the way between these extremes must be graded whatever else in the world is subject to heat or cold.

See another example in light and darkness. They are in exact contrast. Their work goes out from one initial point, but in opposite directions. The supremacy of the one is a triumph over the other. They cannot both be supremely manifested in the same place at the same time, and there is somewhere the highest created light; and, somewhere at the extreme opposite of this, the deepest existing darkness; and, there is always, somewhere, a seemingly neutral point, where we cannot tell which is for the time prevailing over the other; but when their extremes are reached we know that between the two all other degrees of light or darkness must be discovered. For we know that light, as a force in nature, tends to make things visible; and darkness, its opposite force in nature, tends to make things invisible.

There is no evidence that the law principles that are always producing opposite results in matter according to its preparedness for opposite laws. There is no evidence that this principle which extends all the way through the science of matter does not extend also beyond and above matter. We see in morals the same rule of opposites and contrasts. All unlikenesses have their extremes apart, and their up and down grades to and from each other in morals in a manner similar to what we always see in matter.

Truth and lying are exact opposites that run apart in works and character to the farthest extremes of conduct and character. Truth makes knowledge possible to us and faith reasonable, while lying, the exact opposite of truth, makes knowledge impossible to us and faith unreasonable. To believe known lies, if it were possible, would be suicide to reason and confusion to all our mental faculties. Lies are the negatives of truth, and need the negatives of our faith. To finite minds there is a neutral ground where a deviation from the truth may be so slight and unintentional as to leave a doubt of its real place and character, but when the art and habit of lying has taken a moral agent down to the lowest depths of falsity, so that its opposite to truth can go no farther, there is a long space between them filled all the way with agents ranged and graded as to degrees of truthfulness or untruthfulness as the opposites recede from the neutral line at which both started.

So of love and hate—they are exact opposites in the hearts of men. Love makes mutual gladness possible for one and the same event for all who have the same love. Its contrast is hate, which makes mutual gladness impossible for one and the same event among those who hate **one** another. The tendencies of the **two laws are to** the extreme opposites of each other. **Yet** there is, to finite minds, a neutral ground somewhere, **in** which a person may not know **to which** of the two opposites **he** yields his own heart **as a loyal** subject; **yet no one can be on** both sides at one and the same time. The Saviour seems to have used **the word hate with** this exactness **to law when He used** it to include whoever **may be in nearest proximity to the** law **of love to Him, but not under it or** obedient to it. Luke 14-26. **Mat. 6-24.** "No man can serve two masters; **for either he** will hate the one and love the other, or else **he** will hold to the one and despise the other. **Ye cannot serve God** and Mammon." Love **and hate are opposite laws** going out in opposite **directions towards** opposite ends from the one human heart and mind, and no person can follow both **of** these laws in re**spect to** the **same** object at **the** same time. While this is self evident, it **is** not always recognized by persons who do not feel any hatred toward the object considered, and probably will not until a trial or temptation is presented to the mind so as to move it to assert its real affection either for or against the object or person considered.

If we examine other laws of the heart and mind in the same manner regarding their opposites, a uniformity of principle will appear among them all. All have their opposites. The law of faith has its opposite in unbelief—in no faith. No person can respond to both these laws in respect to the same object at the same time. The one law is fulfilled in the reliance of the mind upon propositions considered as true, and the other rejects the same propositions as false; so that any person not conscious of either faith or unbelief, or of either accepting or rejecting as true any of the propositions considered, may not know to which law he is responding, until the temptation or trial of his faith is made, and whatever conduct follows the trial will show whether he is of faith or of unbelief in respect to the proposition considered.

Faith is such an important law of our hearts and minds that it is always worth while to know exactly what we mean by the word, or what the law is we keep when we have faith. It has been said, and well said, that—"Faith is a dependence on the veracity of another." But what is it that the soul does to place itself in a state of dependence upon another? How can the soul know it has faith? What is faith to the believer himself? To this question we answer—Faith is an act of the whole mind as a unit. It is not an act of the will nor of the understanding, nor an act of the judgment, nor of the affections, nor of the conscience, nor an act of the perceptive faculties, nor an act of the memory, nor an act of refined taste and sentiment; but it is the agreement of the whole mind in the absolute veracity and trustworthiness of the author of its own convictions. All the faculties of the mind have their preliminary work in leading up to this supreme agreement of itself in all its acts of true faith. The will helps the mind to seek patiently for the truth; it wills the mind to be impartial and thorough in obtaining testimony, and reason makes fair and true discrimination in the same. The judgment decides the weight of evidence, and faith comes from the agreement of all these. It is a simple and distinct act of the whole heart and mind, as one act by one mind reposing its trust upon some other mind or reality as true, and therefore of complete trustworthiness. The immediate object of faith before the mind is perfect truth, even when it is apprehended as a personal subject. If I believe in God, it is because my whole soul reposes upon Him as a true, personal and trustworthy being. Let faith be an act of the whole mind and not a part of it; and the immediate object of faith be truth, which may be in a person who has convinced us of his perfect veracity and trustworthiness, so that we can and do reply upon that veracity without fear of its failure. Nothing but a false faith can come from efforts at willing the mind to believe evidences that are not clear and conclusive, and of force to carry conviction to the whole mind in its perfect and entire integrity. It is not reason to try and use our faith as we do our eyes to look where we please. Our faith should go with the truths proven to us and never from such truths and proofs. Religion is never honored by a chaffy faith that floats in "every wind of doctrine," nor by a medical prescription faith that is peddled about town for money and taken as a panacea for physical diseases, nor by any wonders of faith that would see some mysterious relic of the past—the bones of reputed saints performing miracles. But actual, genuine faith, resting in the whole truth, has the support of all the intelligent faculties of our minds, acting in harmonious agreement. It leads the whole soul to all its truly hopeful efforts. When its object is our Divine Lord, it raises the human to the divine will, and establishes the fact of "righteousness and peace and joy in the Holy Ghost." Without faith the mind is without an intelligent self-leadership, and can decide upon no reasonable plan of effort ; neither can it have any reasonable plan for any effort, to do it knows not and believes not what. Man was not made to project his way through this world without faith, and it does matter what men believe. "Buy the truth and sell it not." —Prov. 23-23.

All the laws of nature are practically omnipresent ; that is, we know of no place where they are not. If we take the law of gravitation and start out to find some place where it is not, our search will be in vain. There is no such place. The whole science of Astronomy is based on the universality of the law of gravitation. The planetary worlds and the sidereal heavens, all suns and moons and stars, wherever we see them in the universe, give prompt and exact obedience to the law of gravitation. They are all subjects of that law. All eclipses of planets and stars are calculated and predicted for thousands of years to come on that law. But gravitation is a dependent law, and never moves any matter that is not prepared for its hold upon it and kept in order so to continue. It never acts alone. The law of cohesion is always manifested in holding the atoms together in solids for gravitation to take on their circuits through space. So these two laws are never manifested separately. Neither is any other law of nature manifested alone. The presence of repulsion is implied wherever cohesion is seen, and cohesion must hold together whatever gravitation is carrying along through space. So there are interdependencies of many kinds all through the laws of nature, and a fair deduction will concede the omnipresence of the whole system of the laws of nature, and of each one in particular. There is no place where the law is not, and its manifestations are to be expected wherever there is any matter to receive it—made ready to receive it.

The presence of a law and its manifestations are two distinct things, not to be confounded. A law against stealing may extend all the time over the whole State, but its presence is manifested when a thief is punished for his crime, in whatever part of the State he may have been caught, for he could not steal in the State but where the law forbade it. And so the law of gravitation extends throughout the universe, and is manifested wherever there is any object or matter made ready to receive it. Take matter prepared for it to any place in the universe, and you will find the law there as certainly as it is here. Whenever a new world is rightly conditioned in any part of space, for any given law of nature, as the law of gravitation, that law is present and takes its new burden upon just the same terms as all other previously made worlds have been taken, and with infinitely exact adjustments.

The laws of nature regarded as acts of God, permeating all space and all atoms of matter throughout the universe, teach us that our Heavenly Father's plan for the conduct of this and all other worlds is a plan of government by laws; and we cannot find an atom of matter anywhere that is not under infinite and omnipresent laws, even in the conditions upon which atoms of matter pass from one law to another.

In all departments of divine government whatever is prepared for a higher law has it. The most obvious thing in the material world is that matter always goes at once where it is made ready to go, and it goes there under the infinite force that enforces law. When you would fall a tree to the north you chop it on the north side, and when to the south on the south side, and the law of gravitation is present there, and the unseen in nature obeys it and brings down the tree on the side you prepared it to fall; if to the north to the north it is, and if to the south to the south it falls. There is no fitful, uncertain, partial and unreliable law in all the divine system of laws revealed to men. They perform what they promise without respect of persons.

Yet, with all this, a special providence and answers to prayers are both reasonable and natural. Yea, more reasonable than they could be if we had found the laws of nature in material atoms variable, and given to habitual discriminations. For now our prayer goes not to the laws, but to "our Father which art in Heaven," who made this world with all its faithful laws for our use and can make another if there is any need of it. We have these laws plus God, Himself! One of the Divine methods of answering prayer is by a gracious work in our own hearts, by which we are fitted for a higher law of trust in Him, and thus made free from many anxieties about things beyond our control. Our faith and love cast out fear. We offer no dictation to Him, but try to render a prompt and faithful performance of what we believe to be our duties. God may influence us or some other person and leave even an enemy disinclined to do us harm. This we know, that **the Creator and Author of** such just laws **must be able** and willing **to** answer **all filial prayer that goes up to Him in** trust **of His word and love, and from hearts** hungering and thirsting to know **and to do His** own Holy Will. **Let** us offer all the prayers that **are exactly** in the line of obedience to God **and** good will **to men:** "**To** do good and **to** communicate, **for** with such sacrifices God is well pleased."—Heb. 13-16.

The world is always busy with the prayers of men from one to another; **and the idea that** He, who made **the** world, cannot **answer a** reasonable prayer **is** inconsistent **with** perfection of character.

There is a manifest law **of prayer between God and men,** and whenever **we are conditioned and made** entirely **ready for any given prayer, it will be** heard and answered as is best for us. "**Prayer** tests," **proposed to** the praying believers **in God by people who do not pray themselves, if seriously** attempted, would be profane. We **do not owe** any experiments with God for the entertainment of unbelievers. Our religion should go more reverently to God, and our good will to men will be better shown by a manlier dignity of character toward them, while we are walking humbly with God. All Christians have evidence of answers to their prayers, or they would still be without hope in Christ; yet Christians are second to none in their belief of the universality and permanency of all the Divine Laws.

True science justly claims to be always in accord with all the laws of nature, but true religion claims much more—not only perfect accord with all the laws of nature, but with all the laws of Divine revelation also. "To the law and the testimony, if they speak not according to this word, it is because there is no light in them."—Is. 8-20.

No finite mind may be able to tell precisely what degree of moral freedom he enjoys, or what is possible to be done by his own self-agency. We all know, however, that the Divine government in both nature and revelation is calling all moral beings more and more earnestly to use their freedom in resisting evil and striving more earnestly for the attainment of the highest good. At every advanced step of knowledge new fields are opened, with fresh motives to righteousness and it rewards even in this life. But the strongest appeals are made finally to the freedom of individuals to accept the redemption provided in Christ. Men are covenanted with as free persons, able to value and desire eternal life as an act of their own choice, and no provision is made for moving heavenward unwillingly, no call for bond service. Christianity makes the redeemed the Friends of their Lord and the Children of God. It is freedom of will as well as righteousness of life that grades believers upward towards the perfect will of God in Christ Jesus. Freedom and righteousness are inseparable at the throne of the universe in our Father's House. The opposite law is not only away from God, but it is bondage and sin, increasingly great on the down grade. The contrast is unavoidable in the processes of law; progressive opposites are towards extreme opposites. The opposite to harmony, freedom and righteousness with God is bondage to sin, and somewhere between these extremes, ranged along the opposite ways, are all the self-acting moral agents in the world, either opposite to the love of God and receding from Him, or in the love of God and advancing toward Him. Whoever is self-preparing for lower laws of morals and religion is moving toward sin and bondage in the chains of evil habits. And whoever is getting ready for higher laws by repentance, faith and love to God is moving towards freedom and righteousness and joy in the Holy Ghost, being more and more constrained by the love of God.

Thus far are the calls and warnings that come from the laws of nature in material things. Science is based on their permanency, sees no way for their ending; hence they will never be changed, and whatever is moving at all is moving towards one or the other opposite extreme. **The** finalities **of** all things are **in two opposites only, and between them there is** a great gulf fixed. **Luke** 16-26. If man will rise higher than he now is, he must change and be changed so as to conform to the higher laws to which he aspires, and to which **God in** Christ is calling **him** with loving entreaties. " Blessed **are** they which do hunger and thirst after righteousness, for they shall be **filled."—Mat. 5-6.** It belongs **to the science** of theology **and religion** to place the **subject of** the higher laws— the Gospel Laws—before **men, and to** help them to the requisite knowledge of the **way of** salvation, the way of repentance toward God and faith in our Lord Jesus Christ. Let **men** redeemed **from sin by our** Divine Redeemer **thenceforth move along on the upward grade of life's laws, by** divine helping, up to **the throne of the Father's** House of Many Mansions.—John 14-2.

One thing is plain, the **upward way is** not closed to any except those who **will not prepare for it. Helping** to **keep the** truth brighter in living examples is a work in which all the good in the world may be enlisted in Holy Enterprise. Let simple, honest, universal truth be the rallying call to Christ who is "The way and the truth and the life."—John 14 6. And whoever reaches it first will be first in the glorious presence of the everlasting throne of God, being there by conformity to the truth of God in Christ Jesus, and led by the presence and power of the Holy Spirit, the Comforter, in His mission of leading us into all truth.—John 16-13.

There are all along the upward way of freedom, truth and righteousness agencies in the form of personal experiences, repentance and spiritual awakenings, as well as the example and fellowship of many in like relationship to Christ. They are all working to assist and encourage every child of faith in God in preparing for higher laws, which are always present as fast as subjects are ready to obey them; and to subjects thus moving upward all knowledge, experience, joys and sorrows, all disappointments and trials, are favorable to them as members of the body of Christ. " All things work together for good to them that love God, to them who are the called according to his purpose," Rom. 8 28. Then said I, "Lo, I come, in the volume of the book it is written of me, I delight to do thy will, O my God ; yea, thy law is within my heart," Ps. 40 7, 8. "For Christ is the end of the law for righteousness to every one that believeth," Rom. 10 4. "Thanks be unto God for his unspeakable gift," 2nd Cor. 9 15.

Let us all have "repentance toward God and faith toward our Lord Jesus Christ."— Acts 20 21.

"And Adam called his wife's name Eve." —Genesis, 3:20.

CHAPTER V.

Bible outlines of the first man's life until he was married.

If we could find a man who had never been a child, we might be able to imagine that the first man was never a child; but our imaginings would all be wrong, and the Bible outlines decidedly against us. "The first man, Adam, was made a living soul; the last Adam was made a quickening spirit."—I Cor. 15:45.

Yet, the last Adam was a babe, born in a manger in Bethlehem of Judea.—Luke, 2:7.

No living thing is known, or has ever been known, to come to the stature of a plant, or of an animal, or of a man, without growth. To every living thing God made, He gave food and suitable conditions and opportu nity for growing, and the **making of** each **pair of all living** things antedated their growing. Hence, **we are told** that the "**waters** brought **forth,**" and God said: "Let the **earth bring forth the living creature** after **his** kind, and cattle and creeping thing and **beasts of the earth** after **his kind,** and it was so."—Gen. 1:24.

And to prevent misinterpretation, **and** that no one should imagine that God made plants and trees, and fowls and beasts, all **grown** up, we are told, respecting them, that **God** made them "before they were in the earth and before they *grew.*"—**Gen.** 2:4-5.

And man was **not an exception, but was made (male and female)** antecedent to his **growth, and to his** education, and **to** his receiving the breath **of God and becoming a** "Living Soul."—Gen. 2:7.

In point of time man was made after all other creatures of earth, **and** yet **not so** remote as to be furnished with food different from theirs, for either male or female. And **God said: "Behold I have given** you every herb bearing seed, which is upon the face **of all the earth, and every tree, in the which is the fruit of a tree yielding seed, to you it shall be for meat**; and to every beast of the earth, and to every fowl of the air, and to every thing that creepeth upon the earth, wherein **there is life, I have given** every **green herb for meat, and it was so."—Gen. 1:29-30.**

Plainly, therefore, man's food was earthly, and by **growing** on such food he was formed out of the **earth, as all the animals are declared** to have been.—Gen. **1-24 and 2·19.** "And out of the ground **the Lord** God formed every beast of the field and every **fowl of the air,** and brought them unto **Adam (not before** they were grown) to see what he would call them ; and whatsoever Adam called every living creature, that was the name thereof."—Gen. 2:19.

Thus it is easy to see that **any** living body that is growing on earthly food is being **formed out of** the earth and out of **the** "dust **of the earth."**

But growing is always a process requiring time. Man (male and female) was not made and grown to childhood, and school days, and graduation, and capacity for law, and readiness for business and marriage, and the law of marriage all at once. And there is nothing of that kind implied in the outlines of the first man's life. But the outline does show that the act of God, by which man was made a "living soul," was subsequent to his creation.

It seems to have been in the part of his life in which he was nearing to manhood. The act of God following it in the narrative was the planting of a garden eastward in Eden, where he put the mam whom he had formed.—Gen. 2:8.

Thus far from the beginning of Genesis to the 16th verse of this 2nd chapter, we have the acts and words of God independent of any acts and words of man, even implied. But now and henceforth the acts and words of God and the acts and words of man, spoken or implied, are so intermingled as to require careful discrimination to see upon whom the responsibility of anything said or done rests. Also whenever in Genesis two acts of God are connected by the conjunction "and," there is a time space allowable of greater or less length; often of very great length, so that it does not follow that God formed man of the dust of the ground "and" "breathed into his nostrils the breath of life, and man became a living soul;" that this was all synchronized. The act of God that made man a "living soul" was subsequent to his creation as man. Gen. 1:27. In due time Adam had become master of a copious and versatile language and the time had come for him to assume all the responsibilities of manhood and of obedience to his Maker. He was placed in Eden in a home surpassing the goodness of any other retreat for beauty, comfort and abundance. God made ready for him to receive the knowledge of "an helpmeet" which hitherto He had kept from him, except by promise; "I will make him an helpmeet." 18 v. The female had been brought up separately from the male but not less liberally or suitably educated. Adam was qualified to give original and appropriate names to all animals and to other things as well, demonstrating the excellency of his natural and acquired abilities. And the female was not less of an exalted nature and accomplished for the very highest earthly companionship to which she had been appointed of God, and was "made" manifest in due time and God "brought her to the man." Gen. 2 : 22.

We must not forget or omit to see now and henceforth that the words and acts of man are so intermingled with the words and acts of God as to give a divided responsibility for the narrative before us considered as a whole.

Adam's contribution must be carefully considered. Adam said, "This is now bone of my bone, and flesh of my flesh." This implies that he takes upon himself the responsibility or adoption of what immediately precedes his own speech. We find good evidence that **God** did not bring the woman **to Adam** until he had provided suitably for them both in Eden, **and was** ready to see them married and to bestow His blessing. Adam had desired a helpmeet. And if we suppose the exuberance of the human imagination in its pristine state and **in the joy of receiving "an** helpmeet."

So unexpectedly and suddenly and of such surpassing **fitness to** himself could enable him to **account for the Lord's** bringing a mate to him by the way of **such a unique** process of manufacture more **readily than** by any other way. Then this hard part of **the narrative, this** metaphor, this rib story, is all accounted for, **and Adam is responsible for sending down to us this** enigmatical **account of the** origin of woman. Perhaps he did not imagine it **would ever be** interpreted literally. **No Bible writer ever recognized it. Our Saviour wholly disregarded it, and referred directly to the identical persons, male and female, that God first** made as the actual couple that are now united in marriage. If there was any mystery, he has brushed it aside and made the occasion of that first marriage God's time of giving to man the true law of marriage for all men and for all time. "And He answered and said unto them, 'Have ye not read that He which made them at the beginning made them male and female. And said, for this cause shall a man leave father and mother and shall cleave to his wife : and they twain shall be one flesh! Wherefore they are no more twain but one flesh. What therefore God hath joined together let not man put asunder.'" Matt. 19 : 4-6.

www.ingramcontent.com/pod-product-compliance
Lightning Source LLC
Chambersburg PA
CBHW032156160426
43197CB00008B/944